SOVEREIGNTY

&

REMEMBRANCE

Mwalimu K. Bomani Baruti

Copyright © 2015 Larry D. Crawford

All rights reserved. No part of this publication may be reproduced, stored in a retrieval system or transmitted in any form or by any means electronic, mechanical or otherwise without the prior written permission of the publisher.

ISBN: 978-1507638019

Text and Cover formatting by Afia Raina Turner.
Cover photo by Haiwa Nefer Atum.
Ntoreasee Otuko diagram formatted by Boukman Sankofa.

Akoben House
P.O. Box 10786
Atlanta, Georgia 30310

www.AkobenHouse.com

to

HUMZAH

TABLE OF CONTENTS

INTRODUCTION	1
SOVEREIGNTY	5
REMEMBRANCE	57
ENDNOTES	97

INTRODUCTION

We cannot obtain sovereignty without first identifying and mastering the power required to create and sustain it. However, accessing, mobilizing and exercising our power toward this goal is not as difficult a process as it may seem if we take the time to look for it within ourselves and tap into our ancestral memory.

The two essays within *Sovereignty & Remembrance* address the need for doing this preliminary, visionary, nationbuilding work. Both give us ample reason to reflect on the meaning and importance of power and memory and why they will need to be seriously reconsidered by our Warriors if Afrikan people are to again become whole.

The initial essay, "Sovereignty," does three things. First, it offers a working definition of this elusive, often misdefined, concept. We must know where we are trying to go and what we are trying to attain. Second, it looks at exactly what would be required for us to restore sanity to Afrikan people. We must know what is required for us to do so. And, finally, it goes on to address, in specific, practical terms, the question of what we can be doing at this moment to reach this very possible and necessary goal. For, if we do not act now, the opportunity may not arise again.

"Remembrance," the second essay, discusses how one piece of our Maafa ("Great Destruction"), our capture and enslavement, must be thoroughly considered if we are to attain sovereignty. In truth, it is designed to illustrate where we have yet to physically, mentally, emotionally and spiritually go before seriously tackling our liberation, empowerment and sovereignty in any meaningful, realistic, lasting way.

As an introduction to this thinking process, Remembrance offers a broader, more comprehensive, view of the idea of reparations. But it is more than simply an intellectual exercise because it serves as a guide to the kind of ourstorically-grounded worldview Warriors must have if we are going to be able to clearly understand the magnitude of the work which will be required to fulfill our individual and collective missions.

The cover photo is of a meditative activity in Njideka Karmo's "Journey Into Wombmanhood" rites program. Here she is guiding some of the community daughters through a meditation into their power and the responsibility of using that potential in service to Afrikan people through her. It represents the work being done now all over the PanAfrikan world to transfer the heart and soul of who we are and have always been from one generation to the next.

The stars blanketing the entire cover's background speak to the boundless possibilities of Afrikan sovereignty. For, as Listervelt Middleton once penned, "...no man or woman that is free to chase stars is satisfied with chasing a ball." Nothing that we cannot remove from our way stands between us and the highest level of existence, the ultimate human condition – sovereignty.

For this work, I would like to acknowledge the immeasurable, loving assistance of my wife Ena Yaa Mawusi Baruti whose dedication to, and sacrifice for, this work for our people is unparalleled by any other in my life. Her centered advice on these issues over the decades, and meticulous editing skills in this and all of my writings, are second to none. I would also like to say Meda ase piii to

Marimba Ani, a phenomenal jegna who repeatedly articulates our need for unqualified sovereignty and who has uncompromisingly conceptualized and contextualized this vision of a liberated, empowered, sane Afrikan mind. A special Meda ase piii is extended to Afia Raina Turner. Beyond the presence of her bright Warrior spirit in our lives, her commitment, diligence and perseverance has been of immeasurable technical value in this project.

SOVEREIGNTY

> No race is free until it has a strong nation of its own; its own system of government and its own order of society. Never give up this idea. Let no one persuade you against it. It is the only protection for your generation and your race.
>
> *Marcus Mosiah Garvey*

In 1971, Sam Yette wrote a book entitled *The Choice*.[1] In it, he issued what can only be interpreted as a Warrior's challenge. For us, his charge is simple. Do we want to be whited out of existence, or do we want to make a stand, an Afrikan stand, and permanently liberate, empower and make Afrikan people sovereign?

His question remains as relevant today as then. And, at least in my opinion, this charge remains largely unanswered by many of those who would identify themselves as members of the new vanguard.

Looking around the world, it is obvious that we have not yet quite decided whether we want to confront and end the Maafa[2] or continue to actively contribute to our people's demise. In case the question exists, know that there is no middle ground, no neutral corner where one can hide in this war.

Strangely, to some degree, even within the general

"conscious" community there are many whose words and actions betray this crippling indecision. They, too, fear being the uncompromised Warriors they were brought here to model because they do not truly know self.

Apparently, even many of those who stand at the center of the conscious community have not quite fully decided to be the Warriors we need to decisively end this war against Afrikan people either. Those who make up the innermost circle[3] are supposed to be frontline models of sovereignists.[4] We are supposed to be the leaders who are "nearest the enemy, in pursuit."[5] However, as of yet, our lead is barely discernible from the rest.

Given the progressively worsening state of Afrikans globally, it is difficult to assess why this indecision continues to persist. It is beyond troubling in terms of the potentially negative consequences. When looking back ourstorically,[6] it brings to mind Khakheper-Ra-Soneb's heartrending grief over his people's situation.

> I meditate on what has happened, on the things which have come to pass throughout the land. Changes are taking place and it is not like last year. One year is more troublesome than the next. The land is in turmoil, and being destroyed. Maat, righteousness and order, has been cast out and Isfet, evil and chaos, is in the Council Hall. The way of God is violated and His commandments are brushed aside. The land is in turmoil and there is mourning everywhere…Every day that dawns brings events from which the face is forced to turn. I speak out strongly against it. My limbs are heavy laden and my heart is heavy with grief. It is painful not to speak about it.[7]

Having to watch our people being ever more consumed by the full weight of an internalized, fatalist mentality, while willfully, though, for most, ignorantly so, wallowing in a fear-driven defeatism, breaks the Warrior's heart.

An affirmative, constructive decision to become independently empowered can only truly become evident through concrete action. And, knowing this brings to mind another deeply profound thought for those who realize that they have no choice but to make a choice. It is a critical awakening phrased by an unknown Warrior who realized that he had to make the right choice or lose his sanity. He said,

> *So we stand here on the edge of hell and look out on the world and wonder...what we gonna do in the face of what we remember?*

Here and now, in this dehumanized, anti-Afrikan reality, we are indeed standing on the edge of hell. Some might even correctly argue that we are not standing on the edge of hell but in the center of it. They would see us as Warriors who know that we are here to save our people, anxiously looking for ways to establish sovereignty in a world inspired and created by yurugu's[8] chaotic madness. We are faced with the choice between becoming sovereign or remaining irrelevant to human existence.

Knowing who we are, though, knowing that we are our Ancestors, we should not be facing this question. Truthfully, if we are who we say we are, there should not even be a question of this nature. Obviously, the problem lies within us. Either we have not placed sovereignty at the center of our vision, or we have given it no serious thought at all.

In the imaginations of many claiming consciousness, they are actually earnestly seeking a revolutionary path to freedom or liberation. However, the question we most often neglect to ask and answer, from an uncompromising, nationalist, sovereignty-seeking stance, is freedom or liberation from and to do what?

For these individuals, the definition of "revolution" has been severely weakened by their appetite for comfort and painless reform. Believing the mentacidal[9] fantasy that Europeans can be talked out of their racism and that racism is a "human" fluke of which the european manifestation is promoted as being but one expression and, in the scheme of things, no better or worse than any others, has turned them completely away from an effectively functional, visionary struggle.

Blindly believing that some yurugu are good, or that a human core lies somewhere deep within all of them, is a mistake only mentacidal dreamers would make. Only the mentacidal harbor the delusion that some all equally-inclusive, global, european democratic empire will prevail. Only those "revolutionaries" who imagine a power in their powerlessness and have the dream of a raceless, unicultural, eurocentric invisibility would hold such an unfounded myth so closely to their hearts. Only broken spirits merely pursue a reactionary, conversational reform.

In momentarily reflecting on why we find ourselves in this situation under these circumstances, we tend to point to yurugu as the primary source of the problem. And this is a fair and accurate accusation. They are *responsible*. Without a doubt, yurugu is the cornerstone of the edifice obstructing our sovereignty. And we should be sensible enough to know that we must rise and yurugu must fall if we are to gain sovereignty.

However, we should also be aware that they are but one foundational piece, and not the whole of the oppressive conspiracy. Nonetheless, it is only logical that if yurugu were made to fall, to be stripped of all power over us, those remaining foundational usurpers of our sovereignty, the arabs and asians (and their, and yurugu's, negro[10] guard), would more easily be made to crumble. For this, for the removal of their domination over us, we, alone, are *accountable*.[11]

So, for clarity's sake, let us start here with a knowledge of who we are not and what we must face if we are who we say we are. Let us begin our Warrior's thinking at the point of recognition, the point when we become aware of the fact that we are in dire need of making a choice which will determine the future of our people.

And, while on this road to self-discovery, let us make a way to move completely away from those, without the capacity[12] or will to think or learn as Afrikans, who want to engage us in meaningless, regressive, distractive debate. Let us confine this conversation to those Warriors who are serious enough to realize that we must begin, whether thinking about our individual selves or the Afrikan nation, our decision-making process within the context of being in full pursuit of the liberation, empowerment and sovereignty of Afrikan people. This is our primary focus, our overriding concern. We must ground our conscious contemplation in the incontestable fact that we are at war and that sovereignty requires victory.

Further, let us operate completely on the assumption that sovereignty is the *only* way that our liberation and empowerment can be fully achieved. Let us operate completely on the assumption that Afrikan sovereignty can *never* be accomplished in yurugu's space, reality or on their terms.[13] We and they are irreconcilably different in every meaningful way conceivable.[14]

Therefore, if we are to be Afrikan, our sovereignty requires the removal of yurugu and their loyalists from our minds and spaces. For, without sovereignty, a people cannot exercise absolute control over their time, energy, beliefs, practices and material resources. Without sovereignty, a people cannot be whole. Bearing this in mind, it is only common Afrikan sense to realize that un-whole nations can only produce un-whole villages which can only raise un-whole children.

Long enough ago, we were warned to "never be a race of servers, but a race of sovereigns."[15] This afrism[16] holds divine truth. And, because it does, our common Afrikan sense should tell us that, without sovereignty, at best, we can be no more than someone else's pets.

By now, it should be quite clear to the reader that this discussion is not for the faint of heart. It is limited to those who are deadly serious in their commitment to our Ancestors and the generations yet to be birthed. It is a conversation reserved for those who want sovereignty for our people more than life itself.

There should be no confusion here about intent, politics or any other variable which might satisfy those whose greatest desire is to be anything but Afrikan. This is in no way an attempt to convince anyone that our sovereignty should be their aspiration. We are not here to convince anyone to have an independently empowered vision for Afrikan people. Conscious Afrikans are not proselytizers.

The words on these pages are just an effort to better frame the sovereignty concept for those who are awakening to a willingness to consider the need for it, or are already engaged in effectively wielding it in the interests of Afrikan people.

Still, in order for us to achieve or properly use something, we have to precisely know what it is and how it works. However, in our case, we first need to know exactly what sovereignty is not. Why? Because, sadly, by definition, sovereignty is the opposite of the state of existence in which we now live. It is farthest in extreme from the way we have subsisted in for many, many centuries. We need to know what sovereignty is not for the simple fact that within the problem lies the solution. In other words, if we listen and think as Warriors, the nature of the problem will tell us what is required to solve it.

So, what do we have now? How do we accurately, through the eyes of our Ancestors, through the truths dictated by universal order, describe our current physical, cultural, social and spiritual situation? Except in the minds of the mentacidally delusional among us, as individuals and a people on this planet, we have no respect, no power, no security, no control, no activated, unifying functional vision, no meaningful existence outside of others' definitions and control.

We are in no position to determine our own destiny. All significant, life-determining and sustaining decisions are made for us by others, by our handlers. yurugu is not going to relinquish their hold over us and "give" us our power, a gesture which would be meaningless anyway knowing that power is not something that someone can give you. So, even if it were an option, negotiating our sovereignty from yurugu would not be possible or desirable.

Some of us are confused on this point about our "power"[17] in western society because of the loudness and, sometimes, belligerence of our public presence on local and national issues, though clearly our voices are virtually absent in the international arena.[18] Nonetheless, presence and volume are no guarantee or, even necessarily, indicative of decision-making power. Specifically, in our case, they absolutely are not. Neither does our involvement imply that the issues we raise are of our own minds or interests.

Mentacidal beings speak out of the minds of their masters. Our Ghanaian Ancestors knew quite well that "the slave's wisdom is in the master's head." His or her issues were their owners' first. And, whatever causes slaves take up and are willing to fight to the death for are not theirs. At the level of decision-making power, the choice of issues and ends pursued belongs to those who validate their every thought, word and deed.

And, as much as some of us might proclaim otherwise, we have made little to no progress as a people subintegrated[19] into western society. The obvious fault in the analysis of those who think so is the reference point, the time and place from which the comparison is made. For most determined, imbalanced, europhilic[20] optimists, "how far we have come" is limited to the lowest point in our existence as a people, that of our enslavement in the western hemisphere. It is from there that they measure how far we have come. The spiritual, intellectual and physical/material heights of our ancient Ancestors on the Motherland and globally are beyond their historical imaginings.

Moreover, yurugu does not approve of the rightful elevation of ourstory in our honor. Therefore, these negroes and lost souls[21] deem them irrelevant as statements of our greatness or a time from which we should measure our progress as a people.

In terms of the sovereignty question, denial of our phenomenal presence on the soil in which our roots flourished leaves us a virtually landless people. Only the decrepit spaces europeans allocate us in the territories they have stolen are considered ours. And, even there, the barbaric actions they have repeatedly, collectively taken against us when our economic and political organization in these places threatened their economic domination over us made our tenure there tentative at best. This is evidenced in the razing of the many large and small Black Wall Streets and individual businesses that cropped up everywhere we settled, and the outright theft of the vast majority of our farmlands. Their "eminent domain" laws make the idea of us possessing private property in the spaces they control even more laughable.

Moreover, we should be keen enough to acknowledge that the "scramble for Africa" never ended.[22] In fact, it is again accelerating in an attempt to counter the arab and asian invasions. As a result, we have become progressively less and less able to claim the Continent as our own.

We can claim no place as ours when invasive enemies are present, in force, and protected by those of us who look like us but treasonously oversee our time, energy and resources for them. In such a reality, we have no clearly identifiable Afrikan roots, no identity outside of a nomadic, escapist one which moves us in breakneck flight from ourselves. Interestingly, we are the only people on planet Earth whose identity is a contested area.

Bearing these remarks in mind, then, just what is this thing, this condition called sovereignty? We have already made the observation that any earnest search for corrective solutions is a deductive process. We look for the solution to a problem within the problem because it is only within a problem that we can locate its exact cause. This we have already done, although superficially. So, out of that analysis, let us now be as specific as we possibly can in conceptualizing this social phenomenon we call sovereignty.

Quite clearly, Warriors have to be very, very precise in our definitions. In a reality hell-bent on derailing and crushing any and every move we make, or even think to make, toward Afrikan liberation and unification, there can be no grey area to lose our minds in. There are no civilians, no conscientious objectors, no onlookers in war. "Every onlooker is either a coward or a traitor."[23] At all times, there must be absolute clarity about the difference between that which we do which will bring us back home and that which will move us further into lostness.

That said, we have to understand the mind behind what we are up against. We have to grasp the depth of the fear that insecure, covetous, tortured, little minds have of our becoming empowered. We have to see just how real our sovereignty translates into an endless decline and destruction for them in the minds of a psychopathically racist people.

We must be complete and clear for, in this reality, a world built on manipulative deception, inexactness invites compromise, corruption and misdirection. It provides the corruptive schemes of foes with "a warm place to grow."[24]

This dehumanized reality and sub-subsistent state of being is not what we want. We desire nothing less than to be free of this sick madness. We want to see ourselves, our Ancestors, our spirit, our Way clearly reflected throughout our reality. We no longer want to be invisible to each other, or to make it easy for the genocidists terrorizing our lives to be able to pretend that we are (not that what they think of us is of any significance). We no longer want to live in apprehension or fear of others' imperatives or decisions.

We want unqualified, unabridged, permanent, national sovereignty. We want an empowered peace. And, because we want no more mistakes, we must define this, our sovereignty, as unambiguously clear and concise as is humanly possible.

So, to begin our definition, we need to say that sovereignty, like every other social formation, is political. It is a condition brought into existence for a people through the will of that people. It is a conscious effort on their part to express and insure the sanctity and safety of their personality and self-interests. It is an expression of a people's ability to mobilize, organize, delegate and exercise their collective spiritual, mental and physical/material energies in service to themselves. It is about the creation, control and use of a people's power expressly for their benefit. And, regardless of the quality of the mindset or character of the people involved, when sovereignty is genuine, when it is natural and not forced or faked, it reflects the strength, will and self-awareness of a people who are in full control of themselves and their destiny.

Sovereignty involves a collective state of mind elevated to the point where all participants can distinguish between wants and needs. Among a sovereign people, the lesson that "he who is ruled by his appetite belongs to the enemy"[25] is well learned and practiced. Sovereign people provide for all of their own needs. As Marcus Mosiah Garvey noted, what it may want from others is a secondary priority and a sharply, effectively controlled appetite.

> Always see to it that your race is self-sufficient; that means that everything you want must be obtainable in your race as far as human relationships will permit. If you are not individually self-sufficient or cooperative in

your racial relations or self-sufficient in your race as a whole, you will have to go outside of yourself for that sufficiency, which will make you absolutely dependent on the goodwill of others for your sufficiency. No one will give away value that is wanted for self, so you will have to serve and become servants or slaves to sufficiency.[26]

Sovereignty is an emotional, psychological and intellectual state of mind. It is how a people feel, see and think about the environment and universe around them. But, no less so, it is how they feel, see and think about themselves.

Naturally, we Afrikans are a deeply feeling people. And, therefore, naturally, our sovereignty would be a direct expression of our emotional state of being.

Sovereignty is a worldview grounded in, and constructed out of, a timeless tradition. It has a foundational source in its people and an interpretation of reality that is created and evolves through the filter of this source. Nothing of social or cultural significance among a people occurs outside the parameters established by their source.

Sovereign people know who they are. They are keenly aware of those who are insiders and those who remain outsiders. They can easily distinguish those who are of the same mind from those who are strangers and/or pose any meaningful threat to their sanity and existence.

Sovereignty is also a physical existence, both of the person and group. It has a subtle but obvious tangibleness, a visible presence evident through those who comprise it and create a social world which reflects it.

Sovereignty is a geographical space. And this obtains no matter how proximate, i.e., physically close or spread out, the people may be. It has established, geographical boundaries, within which identifiable, declared and protected space(s) can readily be recognized. It is land.

> ...it is ownership and therefore anchor in land that stabilizes and gives substance to a people's sovereignty Because sovereignty that is devoid of land ownership is superficial and liable to dislocation because it is unanchored by the life-giving earth on which people build homes and live and draw means of livelihood Because life-sustaining resources are found in the land and whoever owns the land controls life and is empowered by such ownership to exploit the resources for development[27]

Every true Afrikan nationalist's vision for his or her people is impossible without land we can call our own because sovereignty means controlling one's space.

Nonetheless, every individual, whether part of or separated from the core majority or smaller satellite groups, culturally, politically, psychologically and militarily, enjoys their people's sovereignty. As Marcus Mosiah Garvey repeatedly made known,[28]

> No race is free until it has a strong nation of its own – its own system of government and its own order of society. Never give up this idea, let no one persuade you against it. It is the only protection of your generation and your race. Hold on to the idea, of an independent government and nation so long as other men have them. Never be satisfied to always live under the government of other people because you shall ever be at their mercy.[29]

There is no place on this planet where a member of a sovereign people should lack the love and protection that only home can provide. The surefootedness in pursuing one's people's interests which comes with a secure feeling of belongingness should follow sovereign citizens wherever they reside.

We are Afrikans. So, accordingly, sovereignty should be recognized as a highly spiritual state of being for us. It makes perfect sense that yurugu would find it extremely difficult to understand or accept the significance of this fundamental characteristic of sovereignty. They are merely a religious people,[30] if that. But, in the undiluted, unrestrained Afrikan mind, nothing exists separate from its spirit. Everything physical equally operates on a spiritual plane. There, it receives guidance and is given divine validation and security.

As it manifests at all physical, mental, emotional and intellectual levels, spirit gives sovereignty conscious, higher life. It provides the generative force and guides the initiatives fashioned by sovereign minds. Within spirit's womb, the connection between the people involved in building the nation rises higher and is so much greater than their physical, geographical, mental, cultural and social aspects.

Generally speaking, being sovereign means having absolute control over the life and wellbeing of the nation. Sovereignty requires that its people have complete, total, unqualified independence from others. Inherent in its definition is having the right to choose their way, and to make this choice having a full knowledge of self (and aliens).

Right now, as always, for Afrikan people, sovereignty is measured by how intelligently, independently and powerfully we control our resources (including people), story, culture, time, space and destiny. It is to have the power within the nation to control our lives and to control them in our best interests, regardless of external opposition. And, for us, by definition, power is the ability to be Afrikan. It is to have the will to do so and the intrepidity to act accordingly. Sovereignty is an invincible state of mind.

Ultimately, being sovereign has to mean that there is no one beyond us who makes any decisions about how we rule ourselves, how we live, what we believe, how we deal with enemies (whether natural born enemies or traitors) and how we visualize our future and communicate and express that vision. It means that we are completely and consciously self-defining, self-determining and self-empowered.

And, since no nation has ever risen to power and remained there without holding their own traditions incontestable, uncompromisable and sacred, sovereignty necessarily means that we know, respect, protect and extend in time through every coming generation who we are as a direct reflection of our Ancestors. Being our Ancestors means that we, their culmination, i.e., our lineage in flesh, must respect ourselves above all others.

When sufficiently tapped into, our ancestral connection dictates that we become independently empowered by making ourselves culturally, politically and militarily solvent in preparation to secure our way for those yet to come. To fearlessly, uncompromisingly, consciously do this is to give honor to the legacy they left within us.

It should go without saying that there is a direct correlation between sovereignty and character. They can even be seen as one in the same because a people whose character is spiritually, morally and ethically questionable cannot be sovereign in the human sense. Such an organized horde can collectively occupy a specific space, but their aggressive attempts to dominate and manipulate every people within their reach places them beyond the pale of true sovereignty.

So, in our Warrior's efforts to reconceptualize[31] the world through the eyes of our Ancestors, sovereignty must be redefined as a human and humanizing concept. Otherwise, it should not be misdefined as sovereignty. What falls outside this definition could only be interpreted as organized terrorism.

In making sovereignty a human function by definition, in order for a people to be sovereign they must be able to peacefully practice who they are while effortlessly respecting others who have non-invasive, noninterfering ways of life. They must be civilized.[32] And they must have time to morally evolve.[33]

Again, if choosing this definition is central to the

vision of the reality we need to build to be safe and sane, sovereignty and good character are inseparable concepts. Wade W. Nobles' thoughts on this are instructive.

> One's character is the complexity of mental and spiritual traits which mark a people and is a detectable expression as evidence of their ability to transmit their own hereditary information. If we're not passing to the next generation of African children the essence of what it is to be African, we have no character. The fundamental evidence of our having character is that we pass, in very precise ways, what it means to be normal.[34]

However, in thinking of sovereignty, when reading his words the reader may find it useful to substitute the word "character" with "sovereignty" to gain a better understanding of this observation.

That said, for Warriors, sovereignty is the ultimate goal. Needless to say, for us to be the kind of Afrikan nationalist Warriors our people need, we must want sovereignty for Afrikan people more than the air we breathe.

It should be noted that the Afrikan nationalist Warrior's goal of sovereignty is very different in its politics and vision than the Occupy or Sovereign Citizens Movements which are now beginning to wane in popularity.[35] It is purely nationalist. Afrikans having this insight want to build a nation totally independent of all foreigners and their cultural influences. We want to operate strictly from an Afrikan center.

Our sovereign movement is designed to benefit a nation of people, not just a mentacidal, subintegrated individual here and there. Afrikans who cherish a vision of sovereignty want a space completely separate from europeans and any other enemies. And we must be clear on exactly how we define enemy.

Strictly speaking, an Afrikan nationalist's enemies are any person, living, dead or yet to be born, who in any way did, is or will work to prevent Afrikan people from being liberated, empowered and sovereign. There's nothing complicated about this. Anyone who thinks, says or does anything against our people or who is the friend of our enemies is our enemy.[36] Enemies have no role in our nationbuilding[37] efforts, other than to serve as examples of what we least want to be.

Being sovereign, we want to establish and empower all of the institutions a nation needs, especially a military, for ourselves. And we want to only answer to ourselves.[38]

We are not about reforming babylon. It cannot stand and must be allowed to fall. We are about the business of revolution. Our only option is to create a complete and total change, wholly in our favor.

We do not react to our oppression, only responding to the terrorist assault. We are not seeking to find some way of becoming a successful appendage to this pale insanity. As Amos N. Wilson said,

> ...our destiny is *not* one of trying to become a member of this gang of thieves, but to end its existence here on earth, to inhibit its rapacious ways and to bring this group of people to heel!....it is not about getting a piece of the stolen gains of these people but to stop their thievery and rape of the world, period! So it is not about being left out of the mainstream,; it is about bringing into being a new world order.[39]

We have no desire to celebrate some fake, dependent "sovereignty." We are acting to build an independent nation of our own.

Warriors in pursuit of this ideal are not interested in doing anything which does not present the opportunity for them to further test and prove their accountability to Afrikan people. Conveniently misdefined, promoted and defended by those looking to build an "army" of compromised comrades as worthy of our time, energy and minds, those highly individualized "lifestyles" which claim a revolutionary consciousness do nothing but weaken the interpersonal obligations which otherwise strengthen our national bond.

Self-serving spiritualism[40] and wholistic healthism[41] are but two of a variety of safe ways to delusionally survive this madness. These self-indulgent, escapist breaks from a revolutionary reality which requires our accountability to others, do little more than turn us even more into the fragments our enemies need us to be to further shatter and scatter us so that we can be even more easily exploited and destroyed. These pretenses of identity allow Afrikans who naturally have communal, accountable spirits to feign progress in an anti-Afrikan society through the arrogant worship of self.

In the same way, alien-oriented identities are also without substance and inner strength. They do not require us to confront this vampire people and their decadent way of death which is progressively assaulting us from the outside and eating away at us from the inside. They foster fantasies of invisibility and offer truly vanquished individuals a chance at the only peace and love they can imagine – psychological, emotional and intellectual death.

In fact, playing around with these extremes reveals a personal weakness guided by a belief that we do not have the ability to create our own for ourselves. And this naturally leads us to conclude that the european way is the best of all possible choices. Consequently, our ultimate goal becomes to be even better at this individualistic game than them.

Because of the level of discipline required, it should go without saying that clear-sighted, nationbuilding work requires a particular type of Warrior's character. The difficulty of the work, its duration and the people who are to be served, call for a particular combination of qualities, wholly melded together, in one personality. Certainly, individual Warriors will represent different combinations of these qualities and express varying degrees of the attributes selected. But each frontliner must possess the majority of the characteristics listed below in order for our movement to be effective and encounter the least number of obstacles in the process.

Sovereignty-seeking Afrikans should epitomize the highest ideals of our traditional conception of a Warrior-worker.[42] The virtues (and situationally relevant vices) we elevate as most desirable in the group of us who have chosen to form this frontline army should be the same as those we attribute of our Creator, divinity and the best of our mythology. They should reflect what we consider to be us in our most god-like state.

In addition, those of us who consider ourselves sovereignty-seekers' should hold whatever we create to the same standard as we hold ourselves. Therefore, as a living, thinking, self-interested entity, the nation we build and sustain should also reflect the best of these qualities.

These qualities should include:

- a studious orientation toward ourstory and history and solution-oriented analyses;[43]
- a serious work ethic encapsulated in a drive toward independent economic efforts;
- a drive to organize the people, things and thoughts in one's environment and life in a way where one's purpose does not become overwhelmed by distractive clutter and loss;
- a commitment to complements which places an enormous value on having and rearing children;
- a land consciousness informed by an awareness of others' relentless desire to steal it and guarded by a determination to protect it at all cost;
- an internally-regulated, self-disciplined mind able to work without the expectation of acclaim

or gratification (works for the benefit of those yet to come);
- a trustworthiness proven through an undeniable record of honesty in relations with other frontline members and an uncanny ability to locate problems and unhesitatingly solve them;
- a financial frugality which is informed by a "Buy Black" philosophy and well-practiced in the art of distinguishing wants from needs;
- a righteous consciousness which receives its moral and ethical instructions only from spirit, universal order and the Creator;
- a high regard for physical preparedness and combat readiness;
- a reverence for our Ancestors and Elders and an earnest desire to respectfully seek out their wisdom;
- an emphasis on the higher mind and the divinity within;
- a humility found only in those destined to become true leaders as evident through consistently setting the standard for others to follow;
- a wholly dedicated, incorruptible, uncompromising, relentless, knowledgeable commitment to the ascension of a sovereign Afrikan nation;
- a sober approach to reality that confronts adversity without the need for mind-altering crutches;
- a strictly heterosexual interpretation of procreation which appreciates the womb as divine;
- an unqualified, race conscious love of Afrikan people; and

- a political organizer of the first order in the community who relentlessly holds those leaders chosen by the community accountable to the community.

Through the eyes of Afrikan nationalists, sovereignty describes the *whole* social order of a nation. The production of great, divinely inspired, self-aware, thinking minds, safe, loving families, accountable government, an equitable distribution of the goods and services needed to keep each functioning properly and an army of Warriors organized to prevent this system from being corrupted from inside and outside is sovereignty's domain. For us, sovereignty must be understood in terms of complete control over a society's input (what raw materials come in), throughput (how they are processed) and output (what finished products come out).

The social instruments through which this control occurs are called institutions. Spiritual (or religious), familial, economic, political, educational and martial orders are the basic institutional forms.

Nonetheless, institutions are much, much more than simply the formal structures in society like homes, schools, businesses, churches, state capitols and military bases that we can actually see. As we are the physical vessels (or manifestations if you will) of spirit on this plane, these places are only the outermost evidence that social institutions are in place and at work.

Of equal inconsequentiality in assessing the presence and magnitude of these institutions are the paperwork, communications or codification of directives and rules of operation for these institutions. Both their physical appearances and the communications that guide them, bind them and give tangible evidence of their existence are only indicators of the institutional iceberg's tip.

The larger part of all institutions is nonphysical/material. It exists in the people's asili[44] and culture.[45] It exists in the minds of the people. It is a people's collective way of thinking about the nature of certain necessary aspects of society, the purpose they serve, how they are supposed to go about the business of serving this purpose and how the various members of society are to be served by them.

Understood in this way, institutions are invisible hands, collectively created out of a people's interpretation of what reality is and/or should be over millennia of evolutionary existence. They are the social glue or, if you will, the spiritual web which binds all involved minds together with definitions and directions which keep their identity and existence unified and whole. Their sole purpose is to work in every area where those people interact and learn so that they will be able to forever remain as they are in their heart of hearts.

In other words, institutions, as continually developing cultural and social phenomena, come into existence as the people originally come into existence. They evolve to better serve their interests without changing the spirit of their personality.

And the thought characteristic of any given institution clearly reflects the personality of the people who created it. It is the political body of knowledge that determines how people think, speak and act on any social issue.

This is why Bobby E. Wright rightly singled institutions out as the most critical factor in instilling and maintaining our mentacide. In his words,

> There is one essential condition in order for the process of Mentacide to be effective, namely, the control of the opposing group's institutions or the power to significantly influence them. Unfortunately, for the Black race, that condition exists through the world.[46]

Generally speaking, the purposes of the different

institutions are simple. The educational institution has the function of formally transmitting a people's knowledge base from one generation to the next. The spiritual institution serves the role of explaining a people's cosmology, their divinity, universal order and reason for being, to them. The economic order ensures that all necessary resources are acquired and made available to the population as needed. The institution of family provides for the procreative continuity of the people and introduces new members into the fundamentals of their appropriate roles in the society. The political institution governs social interactions and regulates the organization, consolidation and distribution of personal and group power in society and between that society and others. The military institution is the armed force which uses the threat of imminent violence, and violence itself, to maintain order both within and outside the nation.

Every society contains at least five of these fundamental institutions. The only one which may be functionally absent is the military. However, those without a protective arm, especially in this violently aggressive, western dominated reality, exist only at the whim and under the domination of those which do.

Given these brief descriptions, let us take a moment to look at how institutions geared toward establishing Afrikan sovereignty would work because, as Marcus Mosiah Garvey reminded us, "It is through the institutions of a race that the civilization and culture of the race are built."[47] The question of exactly what would be required to build these sovereignty-facilitating institutions in the context of what we need, how those resources would be developed and what the finished (but ever evolving) product would look like, will be our focus here.

The following chart serves the purpose of illustrating how sovereignty applies in those institutions essential to our people's sanity and survival. Note that the institutions are listed and discussed in no particular order. There is no hierarchy here, no scientific separation. They are inextricably intertwined to the degree that we, as Afrikans, as wholistists or synthesists[48] in the analytical tradition of our Ancestors, should not be able to discern any meaningful reason for evaluating them separately on the battlefield, except, possibly, as a means of accentuating their differences in enhancing the power of the whole.

Now let us further analyze the inner workings of these institutions of our sovereign, nationbuilding process.

INSTITUTION	INPUT	THROUGHPUT	OUTPUT
Education	students, educators & institutions	disciplining nationbuilding education	visionary knowledgeable thinkers
Family	complements, family & community	problem-solving training	integrated frontline families
Spirituality	warriors & righteous spiritualists	traditional spiritual indoctrination	spiritually conscious "priests"
Politics	ideology, workers & masses	nationalist political instruction	involved grassroots organizers
Economics	resources, businesses & work ethic	communal business experience	motivated accountable entrepreneurs
Military	weaponry & military experts	martial skills training	prepared, dedicated, warrior class

The movement toward our sovereign education begins with Afrikan centered parents and educators.[49] And, in an effort to be crystal clear about what kind of educational institution we are trying to build, the seasoned insight of

Mwalimu J. Shujaa is most helpful. In reference to them, he speaks to an important distinction between "education" and "schooling."

> I believe that for Africans in the United States (and elsewhere, for that matter) education must be recognized as a process that should reflect our own interests as a cultural nation and be grounded in our cultural history. It should be a process of identity development within the context of Pan-African kinship and heritage. Education is our means of providing for the inter-generational transmission of values, beliefs, traditions, customs, rituals and sensibilities along with the knowledge of why these things must be sustained. Through education we learn how to determine what is in our interests, distinguish our interests from those of others, and recognize when our interests are consistent and inconsistent with those of others. Education prepares us to accept the staff of cultural leadership from the generation that preceded ours, build upon our inheritance and make ready the generation that will follow us....The schooling process is designed to provide an ample supply of people who are loyal to the nation-state and who have learned the skills needed to perform the work that is necessary to maintain the dominance of the European-American elite in its social order.[50]

In other words,

> Schooling is a process *intended* to perpetuate and maintain the society's existing power relations and the institutional structures that support those arrangements....Education, in contrast to schooling, is the process of transmitting from one generation to the next knowledge of the values, aesthetics, spiritual beliefs, and all things that give a particular cultural orientation its uniqueness. Every cultural group must provide for this transmission process or it will cease to exist.[51]

Obviously, because people are the engines in these processes, this distinction is also manifest in those responsible for imparting knowledge in the classroom.

> Depending on the setting, there are three basic types of individuals who formally instruct our children. The least of these are *programmers*. They do not understand the vocation of teaching at all. They are merely nonthinking individuals who receive income in exchange for spoon feeding our children what they have memorized or reviewed overnight without analysis or consideration (or, in most cases, even knowing) of the needs of our students or nation. Next are *teachers*. Teachers give eurocentric information also. Yet, much more so than programmers, they are consciously intent in their efforts to assimilate and subintegrate Afrikan children into european culture and society. And then there are our *educators*. These are those individuals who give knowledge and wisdom knowingly within an Afrikan centered heart and context. Educators are fully politicized nationbuilders, giving our children everything they might need to rebuild the Afrikan nation. In short, as Lerone Bennett, Jr. once wrote[...], "an educator in a state of oppression is either a revolutionary or himself an oppressor."[52]

When we speak of Afrikan centered parents and Afrikan centered educators, we are referring to a mentality. We are not necessarily speaking about formal education or credentials.[53] We are concerning ourselves with the content of a highly politicized attitude toward our and, in particular, our children's potential and future.

Afrikan centered parents and educators alike are eternal students. We are ever listening to the students' curiosities to see what needs to be further studied in order to assist in elevating their minds. We are ever on the lookout for teachable moments. And, most importantly, we are ever setting the standard for good character.

Often, Afrikan centered homes and educational

institutions are as indistinguishable from each other as Afrikan centered parents and educators. Often, in both cases, they are one in the same.

This is directly in line with our tradition. We are a people who have always seen the community, as a whole, as responsible for correctly developing the minds, character and vision of our children to their fullest potential in service to their people.

And though the responsibility of guiding our children toward the frontline falls on the shoulders of the parent-educators, the children themselves must independently express a desire to think, learn and be Afrikan. It is not the job of responsible frontline adults to drag any child kicking and screaming into consciousness. The eventual result of that is fairly predictable. The anger and resentment over being made into something despised will subconsciously (and, for some, even consciously) become entrenched and, at some point in time, manifest in a way that is severely detrimental to the community.

The calling of parent-educators is to "speak truth," "issue the warnings" and provide models of what it means to be Afrikan. If the child chooses a path which is incompatible and antagonistic to these teachings, our response must be based on the wisdom of our Ancestors.

> If you are parents of worth and wisdom, train your children so that they will be pleasing to God. And if they do what is right, following your example, and handle your affairs as they should, do for them all that is good. For they are begotten of your own heart and soul. Therefore, separate not your heart from them. But if they fail to follow your course, oppose your will, reject all counsel, and set their mouth in motion with vile words, then drive them away. For they are not your children and were not born for you. Those who are guided do not go wrong, but those who willfully lose their way will not find a straight course.[54]

If not, those Warriors-in-Training who want to be Afrikan, who share the classroom with them, will suffer from the distractions. This would truly be unacceptable at this late date in the Maafa.

Nonetheless, in order for our parent-educators to instill a healthy and abiding love of knowing self in our children, they must have access to the best tools at our disposal. In order to fulfill their mission of bringing generations of students into full consciousness, they will need quality curricula, libraries, books, videos and other related materials. They will require adequate funding to support enough independent institutions (operating with little to no overhead) to house and educate every Afrikan who wants to participate in the building of a new, Sankofan[55] reality.

The community plays a critical role here as these schools navigate this monetary-based reality. Without its financial assistance, these institutions cannot thrive or, in too many cases, even come into existence. This is where the practice and institutionalization of "revolutionary tithes"[56] comes into play. No matter how small the amount, all Warriors must consistently contribute to this cause.

As would be expected, in most cases when there is a large number of watoto[57] organized by a sufficient number of parent-teachers who are prepared to provide them with a proper education, the creation of a larger institution may be justified. Caution is advised here, though, in politically visualizing and building such institutions. For, if they are truly Afrikan, funding will be difficult to obtain but critical for their survival.

If it becomes known that these children are being educated to *be* Afrikan[58] in any of these larger, more visible institutions, the anti-Afrikan powers that be will quickly rear their ugly, racist heads and make whatever funding it is receiving, or has the potential to gain, much more difficult to obtain or consistently secure.

All monies donated to any Afrikan effort, whether

these efforts are consciously centered or not, have "strings." Therefore, "strings," whether positive or negative, must be thoroughly and critically investigated and discussed for their potential impact on the institution's political vision.

The throughput part of the education institution involves actually educating our children in fully independent communal schools and communiversities in everything we need to survive and advance our people. Such a higher education must include our adult students as well.

However, if it is not a functional education, one which involves the practical, politically directed application of the skills being acquired in real life community projects, situations and settings, it is useless for our nationbuilding purposes. As an ongoing process, such a functional, practical education would have to include rites programs for all age sets or groups. These well-defined programs would need to provide consistently thorough and knowledgeable instruction about each cohort's coming roles and responsibilities.

In the end, the throughput process involves the creation and growth of a comprehensive familial, communal, inter-communal and national educational system. Such a comprehensive system should be designed to cultivate Afrikan minds from before birth to transition.

As a result of what is originally brought into the process of the educational institution, and the thought and activities involved in directing and honing those involved to be aware of and act on their Afrikan selves, we will witness a progressive burgeoning of disciplined minds, of conscious warriors, of accountable nationbuilders and committed Afrikan nationalists. If done correctly, this process has the potential to yield countless numbers of priests who are able and determined to contribute their time, energy and resources to building institutions of higher learning which are even better than those they attended. We should see more and more centered Warriors, teachers of ourstory and definers of our sovereign future, more and more individuals qualified to govern self, family, community and nation in the Way of our Ancestors.

In terms of our familial institution, this genocidal, mentacide-inducing war against us dictates that the individuals in the families who form our new sovereign nation derive their identity from both those they love on the frontline and their lineage. As I wrote in *Centered: Building Afrikan Realities*,

> As warrior scholars, we know the depth of mentacide within our families. And we know firsthand the joy and pain it brings. So we should not try to fool ourselves into thinking that we are the saviors of a people who are fully conscious of their physical, psychological and spiritual destruction but who are simply lacking in the will to liberate themselves. The vast majority of Afrikan people want nothing to do with anything Afrikan, except it be neutered, despiritualized and sanctioned through Europeans by active or passive negroes, or other confused types. On this point, we must be truthful. By virtually any observable measure, we, *as a people*, are losing. "We are a vanquished nation...." This is no shame. We did not understand the nature of our enemy. Most of us are still unable to fully psychologically grasp the living personification of Isfet. To do so would force us to go places, in defining what is and is not human, that we are not yet prepared to go. However, what is most shameful is that the number of us who have allowed ourselves to become duped into being the main collaborators in the conspiracy to commit genocide against ourselves is growing. This is a real and painful awakening for those of us who profoundly honor our Afrikanity. As ReAfrikanized nationbuilders, we do not have to look around the world to see the fear, distrust, bewilderment and even hatred many chronically mentacidal Afrikans hold toward us. All we need do is look at our own families and see mentacide at work against us. It is the repulsion that many of our immediate and extended blood relatives express toward us, and our

understandable, genocultural need to maintain and be a part of and build family, that force many of us to build new non-natal family. We should not have to fight Europeans and family at the same time. For sane people, it is only reasonable to "want to work in a society [we] belong to, with friends moving in directions [we] can live with." When we feel the pain of disrespect, rejection and loneliness from those who should unconditionally love us, but qualify the giving of their love based on our willingness to commit treason against our Ancestors, we must be amenable to looking outside our immediate blood relatives for family. There is no Afreason as to why we should needlessly suffer in this way. The psychological tearing which can so easily result from being rejected by those who are supposed to love us no matter what should never be allowed to become so great that we are distracted from our nationbuilding work. When spurned by kin, we must find ways to create family with those we love, because they are Afrikan at heart and have chosen to walk this path along with us. There is no reason for conscious Afrikans to suffer because we have chosen to be Afrikan. We should not have to be without a close knit collection of caring, reciprocating, sincere family simply because we choose to reject insanity. Family, like the honored titles Mama, Baba, Sister, Brother, Asafo, Jegna, Elder, Ancestor, kwk. is an earned designation. It is an honor earned through a demonstrated, practiced love. "Just anyone is not another person's relative, one's relative is one that has done good to one." Blood relationship is too precious to be turned into a weapon used to force people comply with the unreasonable. You do not keep relatives close hoping that this will keep them from mentally assaulting you. Duress should not be the motivational force binding unhealthy relationships. By default, a relationship is respectfully reciprocal. Having and keeping it is a privilege. Certainly, blood will always be blood. Certainly, people should know the lineal story of their birth family so that they will know what to expect, suppress and elevate in themselves, their children, their grandchildren, kwk. But blood does not give our family members the right to make us feel less than they simply because conformity strokes their egos or makes them feel more secure. It should never be accepted as leverage in the hands of vanquished family members.[59]

We will be creating a new familial reality out of yurugu's intentional, and fairly successful, effort to fragment and destroy the Afrikan family. We will be rebuilding family like never before because so many in our blood lineages today will not want in any way to be connected with an Afrikan nation of families. Unlike the closest example of this which followed the european occupiers of this country's civil war when members of our families went searching everywhere for each other in order to unite that which yurugu had attempted to tear asunder, many today do not recognize or want to see themselves or us in this way.

Sovereignty begins with family. So, in terms of reconstructing ourselves into a viable family institution which will meaningfully contribute to the whole of our nation, the input must include established, experienced frontline families, potential complements, children, Elders, respectful extended family members and neighbors, and stable communities.

Within this effort, purposeful, visionary marriage must be pursued by all adults. A pattern of responsible procreation must be established and maintained on this foundation. And, in the tradition of Kimbwandende Kia Bunseki Fu-Kiau and A.M. Lukondo-Wamba's "babysitters,"[60] wise Elders must be brought into consistent and intimate involvement in the lives of their children and grandchildren. Training and support for all age groups, in every area of family development, will be required to stabilize our family-community structures wherever we reside.

In time, we should be able to witness a significant increase in the number of stable, committed married, frontline warrior couples who are intensely engaged in the beautiful struggle of Afrikan complementarity.[61] Together, they will master the art of rearing priesthoods of children whose foremost priority, as Mzee Sanyika Anwisye constantly reminds us, will be of rearing children who, in their turn, will build even stronger, more determined, nationbuilding families. This intergenerational phenomenon will provide us with the most worthy models of Afrikan familyhood and produce countless generations of strong, Afrikan nationalist families.

    Afrikan people are the most spiritual of any on this planet. We have a genocultural[62] predisposition to be spiritually connected to the Creator (our oldest Ancestor), Asase Yaa (Mother Earth), the Deities, our honored Ancestors and each other. Our awareness of this is legend.

    Sovereign Afrikans have no use for religion because we know that the creative force is within each and every one of us. We know that there is no higher power which religious middlemen can regulate or enhance for us. This knowing is exemplified among the Akan who have no priests, temples or shrines dedicated to Nyame (the Creator) because everyone has equal access.[63] The internal discipline and god/goddesslikeness of sovereign Afrikans stands on its own footing. Spirit is omnipresent and their connection with it is direct and needs no mitigation.

    Sovereignty-seeking Afrikans know that we are at war and, like everything else in existence, spirit plays a commanding role on the battlefield. So, we also know that we are engaged in "spiritual warfare."

> Every religion is a deification of somebody's culture. When we participate in someone else's religion, we are supporting their deification process. When we participate in the religions of those who seek to destroy our people we, therefore, become willing participants in our own destruction. Afrikan Spiritual Warfare is a deification process. Through Afrikan Spiritual Warfare we make our unique history sacred. In this way, we

empower ourselves. By deifying our Ancestors who fought against the enslavement of our people, we are able to be Warriors for our people. Through this spiritual process we become something new. We have an obligation to deify our Ancestors, for only Afrikans can deify Afrikans. In the act of deifying our Warriors, we become Warriors. As we make ourstory Divine through the process of Spiritual Warfare, we are able to use the *Maafa* for waging war against the enemies of our people, as we define it within the context of Victory. In this view, the *Maafa* becomes one of the most significant periods in ourstory, and has the greatest power to transform us into the Warriors that we must be. Through the nationalization and indigenization of Afrikan Spiritual Warfare, we gain clarity about who we are and what our role is in the reclamation of Afrikan Sovereignty....Afrikan spiritual warfare is not a complex concept. It is about courage, and the daily execution and maintenance of that courage in the fight against enemies. Afrikan spirituality is the fuel that keeps our collective engine running at peak performance; the inspiration that sustains soldiers while on the battlefield or away on long arduous missions; it is also what gives a solid context for cultural and historical unity. Afrikan Spirituality through the intimate learning, practice, and incorporation of Afrikan Traditional Systems (spiritual, social, and political) is not only essential to our success, it is the *only* spiritual context that we should entertain for our maximal decolonization, restoration, sovereignty, and victory as Afrikan people.[64]

What this means to us is that without the *assistance*[65] of our spiritual power, sovereignty will remain ever elusive. So, those who enter the spiritual institution must have a higher desire to better use their spirit as a weapon in this war. We must become spiritual warriors.

Upon entering the spiritual institution, Warriors begin to receive a thorough, non-proselytizing, full indoctrination into traditional Afrikan spiritual systems by highly trained, loyal priests. These priests must be individuals who are of good character, masters in our traditions and *who know that we are at war.* In the hands of these Ancestor-ordained individuals, spirit is recognized and acted on as the politically charged force that it is.

Know that spiritual leadership is not a self-selection process. *We* choose. Therefore, in selecting these specialists, care must be taken to ensure that they are completely unambiguous on the question of us being at war and who are our enemies.[66] Otherwise, spirit will be moved to work against us.

If done well, the spiritual institution's outcome will be a well-disciplined, visionary cadre of revolutionary Warrior-healers who are neither frustrated nor limited by the chaos they see in our camps behind enemy lines. They will be, as Ayi Kwei Armah describes them, indomitable, resolute visionary workers of Afrikan sovereignty.

> A healer needs to see beyond the present and tomorrow. He needs to see years and decades ahead. Because healers work for results so firm they may not be wholly visible till centuries have flowed into millennia. Those willing to do this necessary work, they are the healers of our people.[67]

This vanguard of nation-serving spiritual Warriors will bring the full weight of divinity to bear on our enemies. They will be spiritually charged, righteously enraged Warriors who know the god within in the same way as Boukman, Nat Turner, Queen Nanny, Harriet Tubman and Malcolm X did.

The political institution is another social structure which Warriors must ReAfrikanize,[68] if it is to work on our behalf. Here, we are not only talking about the rules/laws or interests we should collectively establish and pursue. We are also looking at how we have traditionally, for good reasons, gone about deciding and enforcing these choices.[69]

In the contemporary reality, we have to return to the

way of individual political accountability if this institution is to work for us. But, until the time comes when all willing and able Afrikans have been incorporated into this work, communally grounded individuals and organizations motivated to work with and organize our people must fulfill this grassroots role. In this light, knowing that our actions accurately speak to our political participation, Warriors must learn not to be distracted by western electoral politics. For Afrikans, there is a significant lack of accountability toward us which is built into them.

A unifying ideology of national sovereignty must be brought in to form the foundation of our political institution.[70] Such an ideology must re-establish a set of guiding principles about how we collectively need to do what we need to do now and our vision of the future based on a conscious warrior's understanding of history and ourstory.

Of course, this brings up another fundamental reason why the political institution, as an organizing and motivating force, must be established in our interests and strengthened from within to serve the needs of those in our community whose fears have led them to suppress their own revolutionary potential, whether they are aware of it or not.

> Another reason for the importance of institutions on the level of the individual is that many Afrikans have become comfortable and accustomed to just talking and not *doing*. Merely talking is relatively safe, while action involves risks. We don't tend to perceive much danger in simply talking or griping about our condition as a people and what needs to be done. However, becoming a doer involves a certain amount of risk and danger that engenders fear amongst many Afrikans. It is often fear of losing a job, fear of being alienated or ostracized, fear of disturbing a perceived comfortable status quo and even fear of physical harm or death. Afrikans have a long history of being physically brutalized and killed for moving toward liberation and this is a real fear in the minds of many....However,

becoming a doer is made much easier for the masses when there are institutions and groups of people to back them up. You will always have the courageous among us who step forward and stand up regardless, but the masses need some support and validation. This is especially true in a time when Yurugu has elevated oppression to an art form not easily identified by many sisters and brothers who have not studied or reached some level of consciousness.[71]

Outside of actually doing the work of collectively organizing Afrikan energy and resources around a sovereignty movement, Warriors must receive a thorough education in the politics, ideology and rhetoric of PanAfrikan nationalist socialism.[72] From this, two things should take place. One of them is the development of highly politicized, local grassroots organizations which are uncompromisingly centered in our Ancestral truth and way. The other is the formation of a vast army of individuals who hold themselves accountable to our communities who are fully involved in producing positive, empowering, progressive change in our communities around the world.

Many Warriors recognize the central role the economic institution plays in our healing into a sovereign people. However, too many do not realize that our economic empowerment will only come when we begin to change the way we interpret yurugu's economic order relative to us.

This will require us to understand that the virtual concentration of our economic power in the recesses at the bottom and periphery of yurugu's capitalist system[73] has been a planned and finely executed process. We have been fully subintegrated into their way of economically interacting with each other and exploiting others, especially us.

So, the only realistic way of liberating ourselves economically from the racist tentacles of this materialistic system is by initiating and permanently institutionalizing those practices which make us the creative, distributive, consumptive center of our income and wealth. And this must be continued until we are able to fully wean ourselves from their economic system/relations and attach ourselves onto an independent economic institution based on a human-centered, Afrikan model.

To do this we have to bring together into one concentrated effort massive quantities of resources, especially including those of our men, women and children who have a mind for business and who possess a serious work ethic. These men, women and children will comprise our input. They will serve as the models of success for others who want to economically be Afrikan to follow.

Materially and monetarily, our resource base is already here. But things and money have no consciousness or politics. Therefore, our focus must be on supporting those Afrikans who have the capacity to be conscious *and* the skills and expertise to handle our instruments of economic power for us. They must be afforded every opportunity to gain extensive training in pooling resources for our benefit. We must consciously, ever heed the advice of the nationbuilder Marcus Mosiah Garvey who instructed us to "never give away your money outside of your race."[74]

Further, a progressive communal nepotistic[75] mentality that leads us to beneficially hire, train and promote into responsible positions only our own must be instilled as a logical extension of their political accountability. This only makes sense when we grasp Amos N. Wilson's observation that an economy is a set of relationships between people and that these relationships precede and predetermine the direction and flow of a monetary currency. Gaining a familiarity with bartering should also be an essential part of their training experience.

But, more importantly, if we are to rebuild the trust required to adhere a sovereign people economically, a trust which will completely undermine the possibility of us seeing each other as prey, there must be an internalization of ethical, nationalistic good business practices among each other. At minimum, this experience should produce a network of individuals who are strongly tied to each other in an effort to build an economic empire second to none.

Militarily, we need all able-bodied potential warriors to answer the call of our war horn, the Akoben.[76] We need them battle ready. And we need our knowledgeable warriors to begin preparing our younger Warriors-in-Training for their frontline positions. We need those individuals whom Hubert Henry Harrison called "intelligent people" to rise.

> ...intelligent people reach the unknown via the known, and prophesy the future from the known past and present. And we do know that no race or group of people past or present ever won to the status of manhood among men by yielding up that right which even a singed cat will not yield up – the right to defend their lives.[77]

In order to be effective militarily, this frontline institution must be prepared to battle. On the practical side, we need those who are knowledgeable of military and security methods and protocols, particularly instructors skilled in self-defense and military operations. Moreover, as many adults and Elders with good mechanical and gunsmithing skills as possible are needed. On the theoretical side, we need educators with a vast working historical knowledge of the tactics and strategies of militaries worldwide, especially our own.

Within the military institution, training must be extensive and professional. Martial arts, weapons training, battlefield and survival training should form the core curriculum. There should be ample classes and videos on self and community defense and instruction in military science, to include guerrilla warfare and fully functional battle plans at every level of society.

From this, we should expect nothing less than an army of individually capable warriors. In other words, each Warrior should be an army in and of him or herself. As a result, our families, communities and any spaces we occupy should become fully defended. This, of course, would require that suitable weaponry be made available for every trained, able body in the community. Secret societies of men and women whose role it is to militarily pursue sovereign Afrikan interests should also be an output of the military institution. At the global level, a viable military institution would have Afrikans seen and feared as a credible threat by any intelligent individual/people who would consider attacking any one or all of us. The power and vision of such an institution would naturally produce a warrior class which defines itself as Afrikan, understands the concept of enemy and is able and willing to identify and confront others who deserve this label for as long as we live.

As we pointed out a while back, Bobby E. Wright taught us that the only way for mentacide to become rooted and eventually defended and championed by the mentacidal themselves is for it to become institutionalized. That is, in order for self-hatred and other-love to take on a life of its own as the utmost priority among the target group members, they must be taught this in every institution that governs their lives. This is already the case for Afrikan people.

Therefore, if we want to be free of this dependence-breeding slave mentality, we have to seize complete control over those social institutions which generate and regulate our mental, physical and spiritual definitions of what is real and what is not. In any given institution, be it education, family, economics, religion, politics or military, every philosophy, practice, and vision must be under our *complete* control and guidance if we are to be free.

We recognize that sovereignty is forged on the Ancestors' anvils kept inside the deeply-rooted minds of those Afrikans who think in exclusive, unique, nationalist terms. And, although nationalism is a discussion in and of itself, it is a concept and state of mind/being which is inseparable from sovereignty. Though the word sovereignty does not appear in this statement by him, Patrice Lumumba summarized the importance and sense of both of them well when he said that "a man without nationalist tendencies is a man without a soul."[78]

Bearing this in mind, we understand that you cannot build a nation with those who can easily see themselves fighting shoulder-to-shoulder with those who hate themselves and love our enemy. And those who hate themselves and love our enemy includes those who fight the enemy only because they will not love us at this particular moment in time.

Those with a clear sight into ourstory and history know that nothing short of sovereignty, the complete self-government, self-determination and self-definition of Afrikan people by Afrikan people, will do. A vision of absolute sovereignty always and ultimately defines the Afrikan nationalist's thought, speech and action.

Given the genocidal relationship we have with europeans and others, in the mind of Afrikan nationalists sovereignty automatically means the conscious physical, mental and spiritual separation of Afrikan people from all our enemies. Only in those instances where trade or negotiation are called for would this rule be temporarily suspended. And, of course, in those cases, only a small number of us would be involved and whoever they are dealing with would be fully aware that they speak for us and are backed by a powerful people who remember what has been done to us.

Sovereignty also has a special relationship to our

treatment in the *criminal* injustice[79] arm of yurugu's political institution. And the nature of this "special relationship" dictates that we define sovereignty in a way that ends our being controlled, contained and abused by it. Therefore, for us, sovereignty would have to mean that only we will decide on one of our own's guilt; only we determine who will and will not be punished for a crime and what that punishment will be; only we give the final say on imprisonment or capital punishment for an Afrikan man, woman or child we find guilty of a crime against Afrikan people. No one else can be allowed to do this, especially the elected, appointed or otherwise employed state agents who look like us but think like them.

To this discussion, we should add a list of what should be considered nonnegotiable, sovereignty absolutes. These are those things without which we cannot claim to be a sovereign people.[80] There is no particular order here either in that all are necessary ingredients in the liberation, empowerment and sovereignty of our people. They are:

- the social and cultural reconnection of Afrikan people with each other globally
- the development of a military capable of defending both the Afrikan continent against any aggressor and Afrikan people wherever they may reside on the face of this planet, as well as having the authority to maintain national (continent wide) order[81]
- one representative umbrella government overseeing the affairs and interests of Afrikans globally with its command center in Afrika
- the removal of divisive and artificial political boundaries from the Afrikan continent
- the removal of the presence and power of nonAfrikan people from our motherland

- global citizenship for all Afrikan people, i.e., Afrikan people should be allowed to freely travel wherever Afrikan people are, especially across the Continent and to and from the Diaspora and the Continent without the hindrances of a system of visas that work to make physical contact between individuals in different countries and states difficult
- a fully functioning transportation system with the capacity to readily move Afrikan people and resources wherever we and they need to go on the Continent and around the world at will and independent of other people's land, sea and air carriers
- a political apparatus mobilized to realize non-negotiated reparations in every form (financial, business technology and facilities, ourstorical artifacts, kwk[82]) from wherever they have been transported, hoarded and profited from around the world
- the actual material, institutional, infrastructural, technological and retaliatory reparations commensurate with the spiritual, genetic, social, cultural and resource damage done to Afrikans by europeans (Old and New), arabs and asians
- the large-scale promotion and institutionalization of the lifestyle, ritual, language and material aspects of our indigenous traditions and an international educational institution, system and pedagogy that are able to incorporate both the appropriate, nonculturally contaminated, contemporary technology and the moral and ethical values and ways of thinking and doing of our people into a functional and proper education for our youth
- the creation of a de-europeanizing, re-educating, ReAfrikanization evaluation and correction or removal agency whose mission it is to determine the severity and correctability of each individual's mentacide in order to assess how Afrikans returning

to our countries and communities should be spiritually, psychologically and physically processed in order to best protect our spaces from internal discord
- the establishment of an internal and external (international) information gathering agency designed to assist us in making informed decisions about threats to Afrikan security, and able and authorized to deploy agents whose loyalty to the Afrikan nation is beyond reproach to gather said information
- the removal of our land from foreign "ownership," control and occupation and a return of this land to the control of and equitable distribution by the state, tribe and clan. The massive reintroduction of non-cash crop farming technologies in the schools and fields. The nationalization of the industries that can best produce those necessities that are essential for the survival (e.g., food, clothing, transportation, infrastructure, building materials, kwk) of the people
- the development of a fair, nonjudgmental, people's social welfare system solvent enough to handle the difficult and debilitating conditions people find themselves in and are affected by which are either the result of new situations and events or the outcome of our foreign invasion, destruction and exploitation, or both; that is, until these problems become manageable through the state, tribe and clan, having returned to their former levels of benevolent efficiency and
- the removal of the prison system as a punitive instrument and its replacement with strong corporeal moral law and rehabilitative, compensatory, service-oriented system of corrections.

Given that this discussion of how sovereignty should be defined has been framed exclusively for the minds of Warriors, and that Warriors are, first and foremost, workers, what are some of the things that Warriors can be doing right now to move us more toward this new, Sankofan beginning? The following is such a list but it must be approached humbly and with a view of the long haul. No one Warrior, or group of Warriors, can or should do everything at all times. The personal devastation which could result from the strain of attempting to do so would prove more damaging to the movement than the positives produced by such efforts.

Therefore, it is strongly suggested that each Warrior approach this list with the idea of modifying it to fit her or his interests and talents. This requires that we first make the time to know ourselves and use that knowledge of our strengths and challenges to develop and adopt a serious, realistic approach to this life's work.

Again, what we do must be thought about in a way which easily allows us to keep an eye on doing the best we can, fully considering the energy and resources we have at our disposal, and on being able to continue doing this work and passing on our experiences to generations of Warriors to come. This can only be done if we remain spiritually, mentally and physically healthy, living as examples of nationbuilding well into our eldership.

That said, we, as Warriors and sovereignists, can commit ourselves to:

- building strong, lasting families. We must find worthy complements and commit ourselves to a lifetime of building on the frontline with them. We must produce children and rear them together into a warriorhood that reflects their divine potential.
- teaching the babies, the children, the youth. It is our place to make them understand our sovereignty priority. Sovereignty must be explained in such a way that it is clearly distinguishable from nebulous, seemingly synonymous, concepts like "freedom" or "liberation." And clarity must be based on a serious

study of the question, "Free or liberated to do or be what?" For there is a meaningful difference in the analysis, worldview and sense of destiny and responsibility, relative to how they see their personal power, that occurs in Warriors-in-Training when this distinction is made clear for them. As we know, sovereignty is an intergenerational aspiration (and maintenance system). And, in order for it to become deeply entrenched in the minds and souls of Afrikans, it must be taught as a philosophy, ideology and political imperative *to our children*. Teaching our children to think in sovereign terms is visionary and intergenerationally empowering. John Henrik Clarke firmly believed both that

> We should produce a caliber of young people who can take on the loneliness of struggle....[Traditional Afrikans] did not do as we do today – leave things to chance. They planned them. [Afrikan warrior scholars] came out of a society that we need to reproduce today in order to bring about our revolution. *Our children should be picked out and trained for leadership from birth. You can watch how that child handles a fork; watch that child's ability to share with the group; watch that child's ability to protect the group and to accept the training that will make that child improve. We should spot leaders early and begin to train them.* We should make a priesthood of this effort.[83]

and that

> For a people to be free, they have to produce one sacrificial generation. That generation

must be the role model for other generations to come.[84]

We should believe likewise. Our children must be socialized to accept as their primary focus the use of their power in service to the greater Afrikan good. We must make "priesthoods" of them.
- building effective, lasting, truly Afrikan centered schools. These institutions of higher education must be solid, independently funded institutions which uncompromisingly pass on our timeless truths and sovereign vision to the watoto as well the adults.
- exclusively buying black. We must fiscally discipline ourselves and dedicate our minds to using one hundred percent of our one trillion plus dollars in spending power on ourselves rather than the mere four percent we currently do. The skills and know-how to build and repair whatever structures (homes, gardens, stores, kwk.) are needed to supply for all of our needs must be acquired and passed on so that as our youth come of age they will see no need to leave our communities and wastefully sell their talents to our enemies because they do not believe they can make a living among us.
- creating secret societies which pursue our interests without others' knowing. What others think they know of what we are doing to gain sovereignty should only be a fraction of the work actually being done to this end. The remaining work must be done without their knowledge and, in fact, without the knowledge of the bulk of the "conscious" community. We have to act on the lessons of the past and one of those lessons is that our enemies are actively engaged in gathering any intelligence about the potential for independent thinking and acting among Afrikan people and using

that information to undermine and destroy any such efforts. They cannot know what we are doing or we will never attain sovereignty.

- financially supporting those organizations which actively pursue our interests by committing ourselves to selflessly dedicating a portion of our income to them. Revolutionary tithing to them is a necessary frontline, survival strategy, if we are to ensure that our organized power continues to grow and work on our behalf.
- forming study-*action* groups. We have to study who we are in order to know what we are capable of doing. And we have to study who they are in order to know how what we have to do must be done in this alien, anti-Afrikan reality. We study to act. If we do not constructively apply the knowledge we acquire then we are worse than the negroes and lost souls we decry.
- forming rites-*action* groups. Our children, adults and Elders must be formally brought into their roles and responsibilities. And this can only be intergenerationally done and built upon if those who are older and have acquired the knowledge and experience be placed in positions to instruct those who are younger and have a desire to become critical thinking and acting parts of an evolving Afrikan community following in the tradition of our Ancestors. Here, as with the study-*action* groups, knowledge and action must be institutionalized as inseparable. And, how this knowledge is to be applied must be based on actual needs in the community.
- promoting entrepreneurialism among all Warriors. Everyone has something that they can contribute to the communal economy. No one is without useful talents. We must identify our own, and locate each other's, abilities and nurture them to the point of communal solvency in everything we need. Enclave

economies (or markets of goods and services which only we use or have a need to know about) must be created through what we make for ourselves and which we refuse to buy from others. We must take total control of the production, distribution and use of what we live in, eat, wear, drive, read, cleanse, heal ourselves with, kwk.[85]

- providing apprenticeships for our Warriors-in-Training and adults in need of skills. The range of apprenticeships we should provide is as wide as the number of goods and services we need to optimally sustain our community (sewing, canning, carpentry, engineering, kwk., are examples of but a few of the skills we need). Every skill that our adults have should be passed on within the learning environment of an apprenticeship. And every skill we lack needs to be gotten and brought back with as much proficiency as possible. We especially need to sit at the feet of our Elders (and even olders[86]) and gather the knowledge of the skills they have acquired over their lifetimes so that they do not become lost in the morass of western progress.

- bartering those skills we have for what we need or need to have done. Trading talent for talent not only helps to maintain communities. If a community is self-aware and flourishing, it also works to build trust and cohesiveness among those within it. These "word is bond," honesty-based, trust advancing arrangements significantly "contribute to the communal economy" at both the interpersonal and group levels.

- connecting with Afrikans globally in the context of every institution we are building. We are PanAfrikanists and this entails reaching out to Afrikans everywhere and tying our conversations, efforts and spirits together in every revolutionary way possible.

- convening conferences, gatherings and other events completely outside of alien spaces and in ways that bring them absolutely no profits. How we get there, where we stay, what we eat and where the meetings and other activities are held should all be done by us, using only the resources at our disposal. To do otherwise is a contradiction in sovereignty.
- establishing security boundaries for our homes and other sacred spaces and enforcing them in every way possible.
- working together so that we can more comfortably learn of each other's thoughts and behaviors. This will allow us to more constructively assist each other in our character development and help us devise plans to better refine our frontline interactions in the face of external threats.
- organizing and establishing Elder's councils. As we do the work of providing the space and time for our Elders to give us of their wisdom in assisting us to solve our problems, we have to bear in mind that, in this reality, our Elders are not retired from the battlefield or frontline. Assisting us adds to the plates which are overflowing with what they are already doing to enrich our community and sustain themselves. Therefore, Warrior workers should identify those activities, tasks and/or personal responsibilities that each individual Elder must do to survive. Then, they must take personal responsibility for doing, in full or in part, any or all of them in order to free up more of the time Elders dedicate to loosening and untying those knots which entangle our families, communities and individual selves.
- actively engaging in spiritual warfare against external and internal enemies. Depending on the individual Warrior's perspective, the divine, spiritual, creative force/power in the Universe must be defined as a

Creator who looks like us, a spiritual force within us or both. We must never forget that, because of our spirit, we are a power europeans still do not have the intellect to comprehend. We are spirit. We are the spiritual collection, the culmination, of all before and yet to come. We are the force, the sword, the affirmation, the peace of the Most High. In our spiritual genes, we carry the way of Ma'at.[87] We, and only we, have the capacity to truly be human in the face of inhuman devastation. Only we have the ability to resiliently tolerate the worst of the destroyers' might. Only we carry the seeds to take evil/yurugu out of our existence. We are our Warrior Ancestors and we have a right and duty to call on them to assist us on the road to sovereignty (but not to call on them to do this work for us).[88]

What will a sovereign Afrikan nation look like? The particulars will be determined by what the world looks like at the point in time when we achieve sovereignty. But, regardless of that, at the level of society and social institutions, it will look like us in every way imaginable.

Only we will be minding the store. And, not only would you visibly find us in front of all of the institutions in our communities and nation, but we will also be the people you do not see. It is we who will be behind the scenes controlling the helm of all instruments of local, regional, national and international power. Only those who look and think like sovereignists, only those who think like we do about Afrikan people, our enemies, challenges and future together, who hold themselves fully accountable to our Ancestors and vision, will be present and accounted for.

It will be an Afrikan world of consensual, loving respect and accountability. All those things which we are ourstorically known for will be brought back into functional existence. There will be clear-sighted, practiced remembrance of our essence. Sankofa will be our only guide.

REMEMBRANCE

"Apology? What words could atone for over three centuries of Black lives lost to unpaid forced labor, murder, rape, carnage, lynching as sport, and every other conceivable form of oppression? Just acknowledge that reparations are not only morally right but constitutionally legal, and move on. Nothing will ever wipe the slate clean; our right to reparations cannot be debated. We are due recompense."

Mari Evans

Whenever and wherever imbalance exists, a correction must occur. Ma'at demands it. The universal way is of change.[89] It is always in a constant movement toward equilibrium, toward balance, toward harmony between all spiritual phenomena and material elements.

And, within this universal dictate lie the Warrior's first instruction. It is to correct, to return order and balance to the way of life on this planet.

Our Ancestors understood us to be direct reflections, representatives and guardians of universal order. This being the case, if equilibrium, balance and harmony do not prevail, it is our responsibility to firmly bring these principles back into existence on this planet and, thereby, keep humanity whole and at peace.

The specific, horrific conditions which are now calling for us to fulfill the responsibility of returning order to our world began "two thousand seasons" ago. And it is an assault which has done nothing but increasingly escalate the intensity and magnitude of conditions which, long ago, had moved beyond horrific. However, within these conditions are the lessons vital to our sovereign development as a people, lessons which are plainly evident to those of us who can see well enough through the eyes of our Ancestors to understand our primary obligation and duty to the Universe.

If we are to become sovereign, we must learn from this experience. And it is only through these lessons, lessons about enemies and lessons about our own strengths and vulnerabilities, that we can become whole as never before. We can never be exactly what we were, but we can become more.

What has been done, and continues to be perpetrated against us, must be stopped and reversed at the same time that we build what is necessary to make sure that this occurs. And what we build, if it is to be safe and secure, must be such that the seemingly timeless and endless genocidal destruction we witness about us is arrested and never allowed to take root and grow among us again.

Reparations are needed to subsidize the fulfillment of this obligation and duty. Reparations require regaining access to and control over the resources needed to build an autonomous stability. They can be a decisive component in our ability to collectively re-establish and maintain among ourselves the standard of what it means to be human.

The material means to this end have been progressively eroded by the most anti-human, dehumanizing force in existence – yurugu. Virtually since our first contact,[90] they have done, and continue to do, all in their power to steal our material, mental and spiritual resources. Along with that, every effort has been, and continues to be, made to turn these aspects of us against us in service to them. This must be stopped and reversed.

Certainly, without reparations, self-correction is possible. Understanding the self-correcting way of the Universe, it is even, as most healers[91] believe, inevitable. What we can determine, we can accomplish.

Nonetheless, that inevitability offers no guaranteed time frame. If there is no concerted action on our part, there is nothing to say that it would not take twenty thousand seasons to return our sovereignty to functional existence. Moreover, something many do not seem to have the historical insight to understand, there is no hard and fast universal rule stating that slavery cannot be reinstated (assuming that we believe that it ever ended).

Unless the lessons presented by the situation are applied and constructively applied there is no reason not to believe that correction will only be forthcoming in geologic time.[92] Nowhere does it say that Afrikan sovereignty could not take forever, relatively speaking. There is nothing to say that Afrikan people cannot become so totally lost in yurugu's wilderness that we come to believe in our heart of hearts that our enemy's sovereignty is ours. Such a completely vanquished invisibility can only be found when we have fully lost our identity by physically, mentally and spiritually disappearing into their pale, dead reality.

The fact that this is a clear possibility makes it

imperative that Warriors move now. We are keenly aware of the horror of this possibility. What has become glaringly apparent to us is that time is of the essence in any nationbuilding effort, and it is running out.

Evil's greatest weapons against the minds and spirits it has weakened and broken are its longevity and entrenchment in them. It reaches its highest point of effectiveness when a people become so full of the interpretation of who and what they are through evil's eyes that they cannot see themselves as other than its inferiors and mentees.

Understanding this leads us to logically conclude that (1) corrections must be made without delay, (2) such corrections must be made in all realms (material, psychological and spiritual) and (3) the determination of what they need to do and become to permanently release ourselves from this hell must come from the clear mind and knowing voice of those wronged. Without this, the chaos, naturally produced in the tragically imbalanced relations between us and born destroyers, waxes and indefinitely extends itself through time.

As PanAfrikan nationalists who are aware of this time factor, and possess a well-founded, definite vision of sovereignty for our people, we have to focus on reparations at a national, global level. Our thinking has to be more in line with that of Marcus Mosiah Garvey's.

Approached as a tool to assist in our movement toward sovereignty, our thoughts on reparations have to be guided by our heartfelt identification with our Ancestors' incomprehensible human pain. This requires self-consciousness. Only ourstorically aware minds are capable of recognizing the depth of this atrocity and the extent to which it calls for a justice that brings balance, not only to the past, but also to an ongoing event. It requires righteously enraged minds which are able to get past the politics of yurugu's self-serving individualism and grasp the fact that this is a nation's act, an act of war by one people consciously and actively engaged in the destruction of another. We have to understand that the act which brought us to this centuries-old decisive point in ourstory, the Maafa ("Great Destruction"), is an act of one nation of people (however we want to define "people"), the european nation, against another nation of people, the Afrikan nation.

Anything less minimizes the significance of what was and continues to be done to all Afrikans without correction or compensation. Anything less leads us down the aimless, self-defeating path of ever divisive and minimizing discussions, debates and agendas about who may owe us and what they may owe. A divided people are easily conquered by their dividers, especially in their demands to become whole.

And "demand" is the most precise word for Warriors to use when thinking and speaking about reparations. We are not "asking" for anything. To ask is to request permission, usually from a superior. Permission is not required. What has been stolen, in its myriad of forms, must be returned.

So, we are not asking. We are not negotiating. We are not entreating anyone to coddle and pacify us through a show of goodwill.

This is not a request. It is a demand, a command, an ultimatum. We need no one's permission to re-form ourselves into a power so threatening that the culprits will feel compelled to return what was taken or, if that is not sufficient to make them do so, to forcefully take back what is ours.

In addition, we have to assess the magnitude of what was stolen differently than most. Our position on what should be included in the equation of the amount due must incorporate both income earned and damages incurred.

When most reparations advocates consider what is due, their view tends to be fairly narrow and politically correct. Even if only subconsciously, they want to consider the degree to which their estimates may offend europeans.

Sympathetic consideration of yurugu's feelings, and how this will affect what they may be willing to sacrifice, if anything, to appease those they have attempted to destroy, is a very sensitive issue for this group of compromised entreaters. The impact of reparations on the pockets and psychological wellbeing of europeans, and its effect on their "friendship," regulates their thinking

However, for Warriors, any question about yurugu's feelings, especially this one, is as irrelevant to us as our Ancestors' were to them. When we consider what is due, remembrance keeps moving us in the direction of more, and more in-depth questions about what was done and its progressive impact against Afrikan people.

Certainly, we've seen the estimates that go into the billions and trillions of dollars. Calculations, given us by Clarence J. Munford in his book *Race and Reparations*, offer suggestions.

> In one estimation, by no means overblown, between 1619 and 1865, slaves just in the United States were forced to perform 222,505,049 man-hours of unpaid wages. The claim for reimbursement for those wages (arrears with interest) devolves on us their descendants, to whom the debt is now owing....[one estimate for given for this is] the 1983 value of the slave labor expropriated between 1620 and 1865 from Black Americans ranged from $96.3 billion to $9.7 trillion, depending on whether a 3 percent or a 6 percent rate of interest is applied....[Another lesser estimate] figured the 1983 value of slave labor performed from 1790 to 1860 at between $2.1 trillion and $4.7 trillion....[from another angle, another estimate] set the white benefits from labor market discrimination against Blacks from 1929 to 1969 (a short 40 years) at $689 billion in 1972 prices, compounded at an interest rate of 6 percent per annum. Adjusted for inflation, the 1983 total came to $16.3 trillion. In view of these and similar calculations, David Swinton concludes that it would take more than the entire wealth of the whole United States to

compensate Black folk fully.[93]

However, even these are very limited in their approach to determining what is justly owed.

For Warriors not fully acquainted with the totality of what was done, and continues to be done, to us, they may sound reasonable. But, those familiar with the Maafa in its entirety know that these figures are mainly based upon labor market economics. For, it is no secret that they primarily look at what Afrikans would have made if we had been hired as wage labor for those particular jobs during our enslavement.[94]

As such, we end up with calculations based on enslaved Afrikans having been on plantations for so many years, doing this or that form of work for five to seven day workweeks (though usually calculations are based on five) at such and such a wage. Taxation of their wages is sometimes incorporated into the formulas but most often not. In the end, the product of this calculation is equally divided among those comprising the Afrikan population in the slave-holding states of this country over that two and a half centuries time period.

What about those Afrikans who lived in the North? Those who were only quasi-free?[95] They were also subjected to the worst that yurugu's racism has to offer us. Whether they were emprisoned[96] or "free," they were not treated much better in terms of choices (relative to those europeans they had to live around – the occupational options were far greater in the North than South for whites) and physical and mental abuse. They, too, were significantly relegated to the lowest rungs on the occupational and labor market income and prestige ladders. They, too, suffered enormously and needlessly. The North was no oasis for us, especially for the many emprisoned.[97] North or South was simply a matter of a greater or lesser overt evil.

Still, as incredible as these estimates would have to be,

if europeans felt they had been cornered into a position where they had to choose in order to make themselves appear the least liable, these are the only estimates they would want us to consider. These are the calculations they want us to remain focused on because what lies beyond is far worse. This is where they want our thinking to settle in terms of what constitutes full reparations.

But even here, our voices are only dust in the wind. In this political reality they are the sole deciders on national matters. Our only engagement in dialogue at this level on any matter is within those they elect to allow us to participate.

Accordingly, our participation is inconsequential because they decided the outcome before the debate began. In their reality, we determine neither the extent of the damage nor the amount due us. And, while we may misguidedly think otherwise because of the loudness of our voices, in their reality, they are always wholly in charge of the solution. Therefore, our reparations demands can be no more than mere suggestions or requests begging for the attention of the inherently racist power-broking children of our enslavers.

Warriors know this. We know that negotiating with yurugu in good faith is a critical mistake. We know of the grand lies and deceptions, of the treaties and contracts, of their patience in waiting for us to forget so that their will, unchanged, is eventually done. There is not now, and has never been, any negotiating with them. However, for those aspiring to be Warriors who lack substantial clarity on this issue should heed the warning of those who have studied us and yurugu who relay that "you are caught up in the discussion and you're not even relevant to the discussion."[98]

europeans do not want us to look beyond the plantation. They do not want us to extend our thinking any further than the economics of forced labor. And, even if we chance to look beyond a simple compensation for labor, to include the dividends that would have accrued over the years since then, they do not want us to go beyond the plantation. They are well aware of what they have done and know that beyond the plantation lies an atrocity far in reparatory excess of what twelve generations of "legal" enslavement would reveal. They do not want us to look at how we got here in the first place.

They definitely do not want us scrutinizing the records (and using our Afrikan common sense while doing so) for evidence of what fines or fees would have to be imposed on them for the murder, rape, torture, mutilation, dismemberment, starvation, confinement, kwk, of our Ancestors on the slavers,[99] in the dungeons,[100] on the coffle lines,[101] and at the point of capture. They want us to only look at that aspect of our destruction which leaves them looking the least guilty. They want us to confine our demands to an aspect of the Maafa that they can "apologize" for and have that apology accepted by the majority of Afrikans who are victims of their mentacide.

In their psychopathically selfish, apathetic minds, if monetary compensation must be made, they only want to look at that part of our destruction which would cost them the least.[102] They have no interest in full, honest recompense. They are not concerned about justice or what is the right thing to do. Their attention is focused on what they can get away with.

So, negotiation is out. Their idea of fair compensation is irrelevant. When we start to ask ourselves what they owe us, the first thing which ought to come to mind is how much are pain and suffering worth. We need to give some seriously deep thought to how we would incorporate these into the equation and at what amounts.

Understandably, it is very difficult for a healthy, humane mind to weigh the cost of a murder. Spiritual people have great difficulty concluding what is adequate compensation for the malicious, needless loss of life. This difficulty is compounded when no murder stands alone and what has happened is still happening. Of course, a look back at what made sense for our Ancestors might prove very useful in this endeavor.

In our tradition, when a person is sick, the community is sick. When a person is harmed, the community is harmed. And we have to look at the Maafa in this way.

However, our thinking has to go even further because a person's murder means more than just he or she is killed. As uncompromising reparation seekers, we have to understand that a murder ends that person's lineage when the victim had not yet had children. Even the potential to bear more children, for those who already have one child or more, must be taken into consideration. As the result of being murdered before one has produced offspring, everyone whom that person was to father or mother for generations and, in fact, into eternity, will not be born. The spirit of that lineage has no means through which to return.[103] Within a lineage, return of those unborn requires procreation within the physical realm.

Overlooking this belief is to be expected in a reality where spirit is not a scientific consideration. However, this should never be omitted from any Warrior's calculations of murdered Afrikans. Warriors are spiritualists and true spiritualists are not individualists. We can understand the interconnection of spirit and lineage. If we are able to grasp the Afrikan truth that spirit's cycles run within specific lineages, that the circle of reincarnation occurs only "within the same family blood line,"[104] then we can appreciate the fact that, without procreation, the connection between spirit and person in any lineage can be severed. Without procreation, there are no vessels into which spirit can give life and energy.

How do you calculate that loss in capitalist dollar amounts? How do you put a dollar amount on murdering a lineage,[105] on murdering spirit, if you will?

And, in understanding that we are trying to calculate these unprovoked, needless individual and lineal atrocities in the context of them being the willful, conscious acts of born murderers, how does one put a dollar amount on conscious, willful, needless, barbaric murder? How do you calculate the value, to the deceased, and his or her family, community and nation, of a person whose murder was full of premeditation, full of a malicious, burning desire to remove this person from existence, a murder that holds no remorse whatsoever in the killer's conscience (if we feel generous enough to credit him or her with having one)? How do you calculate the loss of our men, women and children to just lynching's frenzied madness?

In order to estimate what is owed in such acts. You have to know that mind. You have to know a mind without a heart, a "bloodied mind," a mind capable of callously tossing an Afrikan over the side of a slaver purely for the excitement of watching the sharks attack, dismember and devour him or her, a despiritualized, morally fractured mind emotionally stimulated through using a living body for target practice, a terribly terrified mind that locates inspiration and delight in systematically working a person to death.[106] You have to fathom the minds of born killers. Only then can you realistically reflect on how to incorporate a murderous mind into the reparations equation.

For our enslaved Ancestors, how do you calculate the pain and suffering that went along with having to work from before the sun came up to well after it went down? How do you calculate the anguish brought on by not being able to care for your children because of this and having to give the love due them to the children of beasts who would turn into the beasts who would wear down and murder your children?

How do you calculate the worth of the lives of the babies who were put in the shade of trees in gullies to keep them cool while their parents drudged in nearby fields, infants who drowned because a sudden thunderstorm flooded the area in which they lay before the parents were able to get to them, parents who had been denied the opportunity to move them to safety until it was beyond certainty that it was going to be a drenching shower and not just a momentary drizzle, parents who had begun to run to retrieve them even against the overseers' commands, whips and guns? How do you pay for that? How do you calculate payment for the lives of those who were not even given the opportunity to live even an enslaved life?

How do you even begin to calculate the psychological and emotional trauma to these mothers and fathers over this unfathomable, needless loss? How much would be required from yurugu in compensation to their grandparents, their brothers and sisters, the community of Afrikans on that plantation, their ethnic group, their Ancestors, Afrikan people as a whole, Spirit, the Universe?

How do you even begin to try to formulate on a board in a centered think tank an equation which calculates the debt of this or that amount for just one of those lives? -- just one of those lives? How do you put a figure to that in dollars and cents in terms of that person being murdered and the trauma it sends out in wave after wave into his or her family, community and nation?

So, we should have more questions than we have answers in terms of total amount due, many more. Queen Mother Audley Moore is correct.

> They owe us more than they could ever pay. They stole our language, they stole our culture. They stole our mothers and fathers and took our names from us....The U.S. will never be able to pay us all they owe us.

But knowing that it is impossible for them to pay off this righteous debt[107] should in no way deter us from asking these questions of ourselves. Because something is beyond calculation does not mean that it should not be fully taken into account or dismissed as beyond reason. So, not having enough is irrelevant to the fact that something is justly owed. In fact, in terms of debt, as far as Warriors should be concerned, they will never have enough to pay for even one of those lives lost anywhere during this still ongoing Maafa.

In the book *Kebuka!: Remembering the Middle Passage through the Eyes of Our Ancestors*, I talked about the number of Afrikans estimated to have died as a direct result of the barbarities involved in our capture, movement, confinement and transport during the enslaving part of the Maafa. I pointed out that,

According to Nana John Henrik Clarke, we can start with no less than 60 million. Yet, he also said, that 100 million is a more likely estimate. John G. Jackson agrees.[108] S.E. Anderson...said that we should give a total of no less than 280 million because we must account for those who would have been born during the destruction of Afrikan people.[109]

However, there are a series of calculations which can offer greater insight into the real number of Afrikans who were murdered[110] during this last half century's portion of the Maafa. As Kush, The Black Unifier pointed out,

> We must teach our children the true story about the Maafa if we are going to initiate the healing of Afrikan people. Until Black people know the true story of the Maafa and obliterate the deceptions, as well as the outright lies about it, we will remain imprisoned in mental shackles, subsisting on self-hatred and ignorance. We owe our lives to our ancestors who endured our Maafa first hand. We should venerate those ancestors who fought and died on our behalf; and, we must seek to evoke that warrior spirit exhibited by those who had to tolerate such suffering. We must not allow their sacrifices to be in vain. Make your existence a bedrock for Black justice. Never forget, Never forgive and Never fear.

Of course, there are those who want the numbers forgotten, either because they want to remain blameless in our eyes or need their mentacide soothed with ignorance.[111] But we are not them. So, we cannot allow ourselves to be drawn into distractive debates about how many of us arrived on these shores, versus how many lost their lives in route. Our story did not begin here. Even what occurred near the end of our "great and mighty walk" as a civilized people when they came to get us is most telling about the insignificance of what we have "accomplished" under yurugu's domination.

As I have said elsewhere, what they perpetrated against us during this part of the Maafa was more than a crime against us. It was a crime against the Universe.

> The magnitude of what they have done should never be lessened. Their crime is against the Creator, not just humanity. This is an aggression which has imbalanced the Universe, not just us. In and of itself, this makes their offense far beyond human forgiveness and forgetfulness. It is immeasurable and incomparable in its viciousness, depravity, aggressiveness, deceitfulness, inhumanity, consistency and conscious intent. No other enemy comes close.[112]

Warriors. No argument they or their minions concoct should be allowed to diminish this. No numbers they place on the table less than what our uncompromising Warrior Scholars tell us, and we intuitively know, should be allowed to qualify as science for us. Nothing they say which even remotely exonerates them or qualifies their crime through our complicity should be allowed to stand and lessen the magnitude of their malevolence against the Universe and, through it, us.

With that said, before we allow europeans and their colored apologists to close the book on the slave "trade" (a misnomer if there ever were one given that trade implies reciprocal exchange[113]), let's look at the numbers they are willing to admit and take them mathematically backward through the eyes of our Ancestors.

It is instructive that a number of our warrior scholars taught us that if we want to understand what happened in any given ourstorical episode that we need to start at the end and read backward to the beginning. We have to start from where we are now (or whatever ourstorical point we have questions about) and study the literature piece by piece until we arrive at the source, i.e., the most original causal factor(s). Only then comes a true, comprehensive understanding.

The following chart is based on two sets of estimates. First are the underestimates approved by eurocentric academia as to how many Afrikans arrived on these shores (about 12.5 million). And, second are the ratios of Afrikans who were murdered at the hands of the Maafa at various points during their transport from the point of capture to their arrival here relative to those who survived. These ratios, a product of an overly defensive eurocentric academy, must also be viewed as underestimates.

This does not, and I repeat, does not take into consideration those who were murdered at the hands of the Maafa during the process of being captured. Neither does it extend its analysis to include those murdered at the hands of the Maafa while subsisting as enslaved Afrikans in the plantation systems of North America. In addition, it does not include the numbers of Afrikans who arrived in the Islands, South America and elsewhere. Here, with these numbers, we are only speaking about those of us brought to North America.

I have no intention, at this point, of debating the extent and intent of our contribution to this process because it is relatively meaningless in the overall picture. This was discussed in *Kebuka!* and well summarized in John Henrik Clarke's statement that

> The aftermath of the slave trade might be worse than the trade itself mainly because the major participants in the trade have made a mission out of lying about their participation in this the greatest of all human tragedies.

> In the last twenty years the academic interpreters of the Atlantic slave trade have been pointing their fingers at the African participants, as though the trade could not have existed without them. Any honest researcher, familiar with the documents, knows that the role of the African was minor in comparison to that of the European and the Arab. The Atlantic slave trade was a three-continent industry that affected a revolution in shipping, in economics and in world trade. Africans did not have this kind of connection at this juncture in history; and, besides, the slave trade was mainly a European and an Arab business. I do not, in any way, intend to free Africans of any guilt for their participation in this trade – their involvement was tragic, misguided and not without significance, but the slave trade would have occurred whether the African participated or not. [114]

Still, it should not be ignored as a lesson in commerce dependency and the fate of those subject to cultural disruption and alienation. Here, our central question remains, "How many?"

During our movement along the coffle lines one in every three Afrikans was murdered. In our stay in the dungeons which followed this trek, four in every five of us were murdered. On the slavers which transported us across the Kemetic Ocean[115] one in every two or three (or 2.5) of us were murdered/died.

These ratios are critical in gaining a Warrior's comprehension and feel for the magnitude of our murders. In using them, as the following graph shows, we can see that

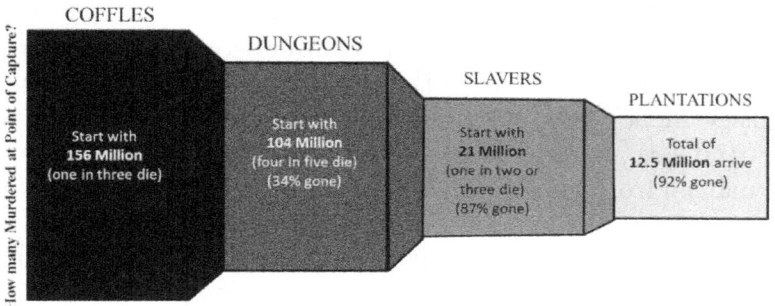

92 percent of us who were involved in this process, from its very beginning, never made it to these shores. 92 percent!
Ntoreasee Otuko[116] Murder Toll Diagram

Given these ratios, in order to end up with 12.5 million arriving, at minimum, you would have to have started with 156 million. The death toll is beyond belief.

Let us do the math. If we start with 156 million at the very beginning of the coffle lines, one in three murdered leaves only 104 million making it to the dungeons. That means 34 percent were physically removed from this planet on the coffle lines.

Combined with those lost during the coffle lines, by the end of our stay in the dungeons we would have lost a total of 87 percent. This means that 135 million of the original 156 million would have to have been murdered before we were ever loaded on the slavers (slave ships).

We lost more family in the dungeons than anywhere else in this process. Maybe that's why murder in the dungeons is rarely discussed, and especially not portrayed in the media. Certainly, it is why europeans and negroes are so determined to erase them as ourstorical reference points. Today, we bear witness to a number of initiatives to tear down these ourstorical landmarks or turn them into jazz clubs for the most privileged of the mentacidal and their openly homosexual masters.

In following these numbers, twenty-one million of us were forced onto the slavers over the years of our enslavement. However, of that number, only 12.5 million arrived alive on these shores. This mere 12.5 million is what remained from the original 156 million.

Again, this does not account for those of us who were murdered in the wars to capture us. Again, this does not it speak to those of us murdered on the killing fields of this country, given that we have confined our analysis to it. And, again, this does not include the Islands, South America and elsewhere.[117]

If righteous rage compels you to personally experience this journey, then study ourstory without the mentacidal, quantitatively and qualitatively minimizing, self-deprecating and self-blaming preconceptions yurugu has forced upon us about this portion of our Maafa. *Kebuka!: Remembering the Middle Passage through the Eyes of Our Ancestors* is my humble tribute to these millions of Ancestors, as well as a way for us to remember this horrific journey we have been cautioned by its perpetrators to forget.

In speaking of Maafa numbers, according to the calculations that we, as Afrikans, have come up with even when using their baseline statistics, we are talking about no less than 280 million Afrikan people. And this is just in reference to that period during the Maafa when the capture, transport and enslavement of Afrikan people from the Motherland and their being brought to the western hemisphere was at its "legal" height. If that were one dollar person, that would already come to $280 million.

Of course, the individual lives themselves would be worth so, so much more. Only when we have $280 million as a nonnegotiable starting point should we begin calculating the amount due for the pain and suffering of the individuals and the subsequent waves that rippled in torrents outward into their families, community, nation and beyond.

This said, we also have to figure out yurugu's debt to the Universe. This is a crime not just against Afrikan people. It cannot be smoothed over simply with a monetary payment to a thoroughly mentacidal people. In a real sense, we're secondary in reparative order.

The primary victim in this destruction of Afrikan people is the Universe. The Universe was made unbalanced by this atrocity. The Universe had cracks and fissures placed in it by this wanton destruction of human life. How do you make restitution for that? How do you fix the greatest phenomenon of all so that order and balance is returned to it?

One of our most brilliant Ancestors, Bobby E. Wright, made a statement in the last paragraph of his "Mentacide: The Ultimate Threat to the Black Race" essay which gives clear insight into how the Universe has to be repaid, of how order is to be restored in it by us. Interestingly, it is a sentence which, for some strange reason, has been almost totally absent from the voices of the spokespersons of the conscious community when the work of Nana Wright is brought up for discussion. And this is his most important essay as far as Warriors should be concerned. In it, in more than any other of his statements, he explains the concept of Mentacide. Nevertheless, the writing is not included in any of the printed versions of his book *The Psychopathic Racist Personality and other essays*.[118]

In its last paragraph, he explains that "blood debts must be repaid in blood."[119] This is not about revenge. This is about returning order in a Universe which rightfully requires that whatever has been done wrong must be corrected with the same amount of force and energy as that which was put into creating the imbalance. In fact, according to our Kemetic Ancestors, if a reed is bent in one direction it will have to be bent even further in the other in order for it to again become straight, it requires more.

We have no choice but to accept that Nana Wright is correct. Globally, every other people follow this rational, order-returning social policy. There are universal absolutes confirmed by ourstory and history. Every sovereign people, including our ancient/traditional Ancestors, operate along this compensatory rule.

Regardless of the lofty rhetoric spewing forth from the mouths of negroes thoroughly deluded into the nightmare of a raceless, new, one-world order, every solvent people apprehends the balance-returning (even if in unbalanced hands) historical fact that blood debts must be repaid in blood. However, today, we are the exception. We seem determined to believe that blood debts must be repaid in forgiveness and prayer for enemies. Then, again, given that we are not solvent, it stands to reason.

So, without a monetary focus on money, resources, infrastructure, territory, kwk, we should ask how do Warriors calculate how many yurugu would need to be removed in order to return balance to the Universe? How many of their lives would need to be forfeited to begin the process of balancing the scales against this already enormous accumulated cost to us?

Again, blood debts must be repaid in blood in order for this necessary process to occur. And, Afrikan people, whether we are capable of understanding this or not, are responsible for doing so. That said, the taking of lives, in exchange for the lives taken, would have to be part of the reparations package, that is, if we want full reparations.

Now, if we simply want partial, piecemeal reparations, bits and pieces of crumbs here and there, if all we want is a few dollars, a new Lexus, Cadillac, Hummer or, maybe, a Bentley or Bugatti, if our desires are no greater than having our college tuition paid in preparation to work for them so that we can earn for them a hundred thousand times the tuition's cost to them or, better yet, for a nonexistent job, then "blood debts" become irrelevant.

Still, regardless of amount, it has to be pointed out that determining exactly where the money comes from also requires a critical historical knowledge base. We have to understand the inner workings of capitalism and how it succeeds through the systematic exploitation of its victims' wealth/income and resources. No part of our reparations should come from what has been taken, involuntarily or not, from us by the state or private interests. We have to look at the concept of reparations differently if we want real reparations, not payment from this, or any european, country which is derived from our tax dollars.

Let us consider a real example of the historical pattern of systematic exploitation of the victims of yurugu's capitalism. Let us take, as an example, this predatory social behavior in the lesser context of lawsuits filed and won by Afrikans against agents of the state. How flawed our thinking is on the question of who pays when one of us wins a lawsuit against the state is quite evident in the contemporary *criminal justice system*.[120] Those responsible for arresting, fabricating evidence, incompetently defending[121] and knowingly prosecuting and sentencing us are left untouched by the state even after they are revealed for the lying, maliciously deceitful criminals that they are. To the point here, though, our attention should be focused on those few cases where Afrikans do win and are given a court ordered monetary compensation for their loss. In these cases, the Afrikan community is still victimized. We continue to "finance our own destruction."

When we get so excited over these "victories," we forget that the money used to pay this compensation comes out of our own pockets. When we jump around celebrating some individual Afrikan winning this or that very minor monetary award (considering the magnitude of the damage to our families and community, not to mention the considerable profits going to lawyers who handle these cases who are from other communities or, at minimum, are politically and consumptively loyal to them), we forget that the money for the awards almost exclusively comes from our local tax dollars.

It does not come from the pay of those who committed the acts. It does not come from the perpetrators of these unethical and immoral acts. It is derived from the tax dollars of the residents who live in the community of those whom the violence was committed against.

We are the ones who live in and provide the majority of the tax base in those metropolitan areas in which we are disproportionately violated. Therefore, the millions of dollars paid out in more than justified lawsuits for violations others commit against us are paid by us. Even if the money comes from the city's liability insurance policies, our tax dollars are used to pay the premiums.

Like those who seek to turn the other cheek in order to model a suffering they believe will teach lifelong racists to love them, we are paying the penalty for being violated. We are being charged for the damages of those who legally abuse us.

The individuals who commit these heinous acts do not live in our community; they do not pay taxes in our community. Therefore, they do not suffer for their crimes. They commit these crimes against us and are rewarded for doing so.

Here, crime truly does pay. The victim pays the criminal. When Afrikans are awarded money by the court for our losses, it in no way financially impacts the european community or those individuals who committed these acts of brutality. In fact, there is no evidence that these individuals are in any way negatively impacted. There is no evidence that they suffer from communal ostracization or by being unable to find jobs with similar or even greater economic rewards.

A family rewards its members when they do well, when they serve and protect them from others they perceive as threats to their safety and sanity. So these criminals are applauded by their community with employment and income for their efforts to beat, torture, maim, murder or otherwise keep us at bay. They continue to be honored as the hardworking, sincere, dedicated agents of white aggression that they are because we are yurugu's enemy.

Looking at this grand deception as being a strong probability for significantly larger, Maafa reparations, we must take all the time needed to study, in extreme detail, any arrangement they put forth to bring this issue to a close. Otherwise, as history demonstrates, we will end up paying ourselves for what they have done to us.

So, from where is the money for these reparations to come? If we know nothing else, we know that, if it is to be genuine and fair, it has to come directly from their pockets, in a way that is determined, and can be seen and measured, by us. None of it should come from ours.

In discussions about our enslavement, as with the *criminal* justice system, we know that there will be those among us who say nothing is owed because of our complicity, knowingly or not. Many of them will even contend that we were the key players in our enslavement. They will argue that, if anyone is to be singled out, it is the Continental Afrikan who owes us reparations. In fact, they would contend that it is we who owe yurugu, not only a debt of gratitude for saving us from the Continental Afrikan's hands but also for saving us from the barbarities of our traditional way.

Warriors know, though, that these misguided accusations are little more than the self-serving ramblings of those mentacidal Afrikans who are self-hating and yurugu-loving enough to ignorantly blame the victim for destroying him or herself. The following words, offered by Molefi Kete Asante should suffice in response for those who want to see.

Africans did not enslave themselves in the Americas. The European slave trade was not an African venture, it was preeminently a European enterprise in all of its dimensions: conception, insurance, outfitting of ships, sailors, factories, shackles, weapons, and the selling and buying of people in the Americas. Not one African can be named as an equal partner with Europeans in the slave trade. Indeed, no African person benefited to the degree that Europeans did from the commerce in African people...no African community used slavery as its principal mode of economic production. We have no example of a slave economy in West Africa. The closest any scholar has ever been able to arrive at a description of a slave society is the Dahomey kingdom of the nineteenth century that had become so debauched by slavery due to European influence that it was virtually a hostage of the nefarious enterprise. However, even in Dahomey we do not see the complete denial of the humanity of Africans as we see in the American colonies. Slavery was not romantic; it was evil, ferocious, brutal, and corrupting in all of its aspects. It was developed in its greatest degree of degradation in the United States. The enslaved African was treated with utter disrespect. No laws protected the African from any cruelty the white master could conceive. The man, woman, or child was at the complete mercy of the most brutish of people. For looking a white man in the eye the enslaved person could have his or her eyes blinded with hot irons. For speaking up in defense of a wife or woman a man could have his right hand severed. For defending his right to speak against oppression, an African could have half his tongue cut out. For running away and being caught an enslaved African could have his or her Achilles tendon cut. For resisting the advances of her white master a woman could be given fifty lashes of the cowhide whip. A woman who physically fought against her master's sexual advances was courting death, and many died at the hands of their masters. The enslaved African was more often than not physically scarred, crippled, or injured because of some brutal act of the slave owner.

> Among the punishments that were favored by the slave owners were whipping holes, wherein the enslaved was buried in the ground up to the neck; dragging blocks that were attached to the feet of men or women who had run away and been caught; mutilation of the toes and fingers; the pouring of hot wax onto the limbs; and passing a piece of hot wood on the buttocks of the enslaved. Death came to the enslaved in vile, crude ways when the angry, psychopathic slave owner wanted to teach other enslaved Africans a lesson. The enslaved person could be roasted over a slow-burning fire, left to die after having both legs and both arms broken, oiled and greased and then set afire while hanging from a tree's limb, or being killed slowly as the slave owner cut the enslaved person's phallus or breasts. A person could be placed on the ground, stomach first, stretched so that each hand was tied to a pole and each foot was tied to a pole. Then the slave master would beat the person's naked body until the flesh was torn off the buttocks and the blood ran down to the ground.[122]

And, once all of that has been figured out, we have to calculate emotional content. Once we are able to fathom an innate evil, a genoculturally bonded despiritualized, dehumanized asilic imperative, a wholly de-emotionalized being,[123] once we are able to fully grasp the magnitude and depth of their rhetorical ethic,[124] we will be able to do so. We will be able to introduce their raw, blatant, willful, sadistic enjoyment into the reparations equation.

In order for reparations to have any real, lasting meaning, yurugu will have to have stopped doing what they are doing. However, we know that will not occur because to stop means suicide for them. They could not be their natural selves otherwise.

Remember, if we're talking about forgiving and forgetting[125] (although forgetting should never be on the table) being the outcome of reparations, then they have to have stopped doing what they are doing. And they are not about to stop doing what they do to us because this is how they live.

This is not a pastime, an avocation, something they do on the side until something more humane comes along. We are their meat, their spiritual, mental, emotional, physical food. Our exploitation and pain are their sustenance. This is how they thrive. Their joy lies in the oppression of others because yurugu's asili is sadistic by nature. So, even if they say, "we're going to go on a diet and plan on not eating so many of you," they have not stopped. They still continue to do what they have always done.

So, there are a number of other larger variables which have to be taken into consideration. Reparations is more than just a paycheck, something that the vast majority of us would do no more than give back in just a matter of days anyway.[126] It would so quickly be wasted on the latest cars, houses, phones, clothes, computer technology (so that we can play games, not so that we can communicate a nationbuilding agenda better), kwk., anything but land, businesses, tools or books of course.

We can imagine that, on the very day when reparations are handed out, every negro in this country, every Afrikan who has been sleeping with the enemy and doing everything in their power to undermine any independent, self-defined, empowerment movement of Afrikan people, and who have committed their energies to destroying any Warrior who is working to this end, will be fighting each other for a place in the disbursement line. We can also imagine a good number of europeans successfully claiming to be Afrikan.

So, for thinking Warriors, we would want to have a way of determining who is eligible and whose reparations should be held in escrow by responsible, visionary Afrikans. Of course, in terms of our sovereign aspiration, only proven Warriors would be directly compensated and be placed in charge of holding and managing the monetary reparations due the majority of Afrikans until they have proven their PanAfrikan intent, until they have internalized an Afrikan consciousness.

In this responsibility, we have to consider the extent to which yurugu has successfully destroyed our minds. The depth of the self-hating mentacide, and its manifestation through the immediate return of reparations dollars to yuruguan hands, needs to be an aspect of the political part of the reparations equation.

In fact, now that we can think about it, how do you put the murder of self-consciousness into a mathematical equation? How do we measure the monetary value of mentacide? How do we put a price tag on the intergenerational devastation that just one individual will produce, a progressive degeneration systematically instilled by racist hatred. How do we economically calculate phenomena like cultural misorientation, other-centeredness and zombism?[127]

We can expect that many detractors will argue the opposite.[128] Such individuals will defensively argue against us that consciousness does not require compensation, that it is complete within itself. They will put forth this nonsensical argument that Warriors need no reparations, even while severe economic inequality is thoroughly institutionalized and even though we operate within a hardened, permanently racist, capitalist system. Their justification will be that since we are already operating under our own independent power and knowledge of self and that this, in and of itself, is evidence enough that equality has, in fact, occurred.

The efforts of the mentacidal among us, in working to undermine any progressive effort we make to empower ourselves and defend our enemies, are uncanny but predictable. But, obviously, there are many fundamental flaws in their arguments. The most important omission given is that wealth gives decision-making power in a capitalist system. Therefore, in a money-centered social order, a core requirement for the long-term, progressive sustainability of our movement is sufficient, secure finances. However, because of the nature of a Warrior's work, we tend to be the most economically disadvantaged and insecure. Still, more than other Afrikans, Warriors need resources which, in a capitalist system, chiefly come by way of money.

Like every other Afrikan (relative to their european counterpart), Warriors operate out of a massive, and still significant impactful, past deficit. Almost always, there was a lost life before our awakening. It was a life ruled by the chaos of conspicuous consumption and waste. This was a mentacidal life, a life resulting from our contact with an inferiorizing socialization within yurugu's culture and society. The planned miseducation which guided us to naively squander our meager resources is what must be compensated for in order for us to do this work to the best of our ability.[129]

The overwhelming difficulty of this circumstance demands reparations for lost time and resources. It calls forth the question of how to calculate a sufficient compensation for the pain we unwittingly experienced before consciousness. How do we compensate for the struggles that go hand in hand with gaining and maintaining sanity against all odds? How will the harsh, painful and, often, debilitating rejection from many among our family and friends, of being dismissed, demeaned and overlooked socially, be accounted for monetarily?

And make no mistake. This is not an accusation. These family members and friends are not at fault. They are acting in this way because of their mentacide, their ingrained fear and ignorance, the same fear and ignorance we had before consciousness. So, it is not from them that Warriors seek compensation. They, themselves, need to be compensated for that. It is from those who are responsible for making them and us mentacidal. Still, we, the Warriors, those of us who are fighting to assist them and every other Afrikan to recognize their Afrikanity and get on the righteous path of our Ancestors, need to be compensated for receiving the brunt of the mentacide they vented against us.[130]

Speaking of the loss of a uncorrupted consciousness of self, how much compensation should we receive for the loss of our names? How do you calculate the loss of a name, a lineage, a heritage, of knowing who you are and, spiritually, of knowing your creator? And, additionally, does not the energy expended, and expenses paid, by those who searched and possibly found their lineage and name demand full compensation? Should not every penny paid by those who "legally" changed their names back to a meaningful Afrikan one be returned in full with interest?[131]

It's understandable why most of our people do not want to talk about reparations. It's understandable why, in fact, they "can't." Except to engage in meaningless, distractive, tear each other down debate, except in continuing to do the negro's work of delaying any penalty to their master until it is no longer a worthwhile issue, do we find this topic under consideration.

But, as Warriors, there is no overlooking it. This disadvantage is not of our doing and those responsible must be held accountable. They must be made to surrender adequate compensation for their atrocities against us.

So, again, our discussion has to focus on the damage done and how to place a value on it in its entirety. A good exercise in this direction might be to look at your spouse, your complement, your newborn child, your other children, your siblings, parents, grandparent, other blood relatives, your best friend, the person standing right beside you on the frontline and figure out how much money, if they disappeared right now, it would take to replace them, any of them. How much you would require in compensation for their lives and for the pain and agony you would feel for the rest of yours.

There are lots of ideas out there about reparations, what it means and what just compensation entails. One of the most outstanding of these posits that a good deal of the industrial infrastructure should immediately come under our control. Claims range from a third to half of all industry.

Another longstanding proposal is that a good number of states should likewise become our domain. The logic is based on the fact that, in the work of building this country, the southeastern portion of this land, "the South," is where we were/are most concentrated. Therefore, this space, more than others in this land, should become our property.

Of course, in many ways, both arguments, the one demanding a share of this country's industrial infrastructure and the one claiming natural rights to a large portion of its land, are ludicrous. They were made as if those who came up with them do not know europeans.

The probability that yurugu is going to turn over any of the land it has stolen, and is fully committed and prepared to defend to the death, to an enemy whom it sees as a definite and imminent threat is nonexistent. It is based on the ahistorical, totally flawed assumption that we are going to be "given" (knowing that anything they give they so easily take back) a space *within* their space and that they will respect the sovereignty of our space. Warriors know that "the difference between the robber and the robbed can only be settled in struggle."[132]

For Warriors, the heart of the problem goes even beyond that. It lies in our inability to immediately create a viable, feared army to defend such a space from the military or paramilitary encroachments which are bound to come.

Even more improbable is the notion that yurugu, who has created a global, dominant, exploitative capitalist economy that is necessarily and aggressively inclusive, would allow an alternative economy, an economy that operates independently of theirs and from which they will not be able to extract what they want at will, to be created and sustained within the space it occupies. There is no way that they are going to voluntarily let their best collection of captivated, conspicuous consumers slip out of their capitalist grip.

There has never been a time when yurugu has allowed

this to occur. They have never allowed a self-sustainable economy to exist within their economy or, for that matter, even spatially proximal to their economy. If we look at it in terms of how quickly they dismantled such efforts, this is especially the case for those who they perceived as enemies and threats.

We can go down a long list of such efforts by Afrikans in yuruguan space whose fate was sealed the moment they decided to surpass the productive capabilities and solvency of europeans and did not create, either beforehand or simultaneously, a viable military to put the fear of a retaliatory annihilation in the heartless, fear-driven minds of europeans. They will shut down their own. So, why would any Afrikan be foolish enough to be unprepared for their coming.

However, neither the lives and labor nor the productive infrastructure created out of the resources and energy of captive Afrikan genius and labor, or both, could ever be the end of any serious reparation demands. They have stolen much of our memory and identity. Those things which we created to speak to our essence and forever remind us of our spirit and aspirations must be returned to us in our space.

So, if we think as sovereignists,[133] as a people who have integrity and are working to again become whole, nothing could be complete until every single artifact held captive in every single european, arab and asian museum, private collection, home and space is returned home. And the spaces occupied by others on the Continent are rooms in the homes of which we speak. These rooms, too, must be returned to Afrikan hands.

In considering the impossibility of a yuruguan "human" conscience in, or voluntary consent to, the making of fair reparations, we also have to remember that all reparations paid to noneuropeans by europeans were dependent on their relations with that people's motherland. The power of the motherland, relative to that of europeans is a critically decisive factor in their willingness to agree to make payment to her diasporic children.

We have to remember that it was not only the movements in this country during the 1960s and 1970s that were responsible for our "civil rights." It was also the result of the revolutionary decolonization movement on the Continent. europeans needed to continue to steal what they wanted from the Continent in the amounts and at the prices that they felt like paying. They did not need the distraction of the Continental Afrikan's anger over how their family was being mistreated in western society. So, they had to make some concessions in order to quiet our rage here until they were able to install a neocolonial system. Once that occurred they went back to oppressive business as usual. Racist policy and practice against us in the West follows this transition from colonial status to independent status to neocolonial status on the Continent.

Recognizing this, Warriors should not deceive themselves about the probability of reparations from yurugu. We would be foolhardy to sit around waiting for yurugu to wake up to some humanity which compels them to right their wrongs. We have to continue on the path of full reparations alongside a sovereign empowerment which needs to ask nothing of them because they fear what will happen if they do not.

If balance is to be returned, we are obligated by a destroyed way of life to speak about reparations as an egregious harm in its totality, not its individual portions. That so, then we also need to consider our losses from the following, far from complete, listing. Warriors would also have to give thought to the billions upon billions swindled from Afrikans by sharecroppers, law enforcement and the courts (in everything from ticket fines to bail fees), prisons (in everything from the charges for phone calls to relocating enmates to institutions far distanced from relatives), chain gangs, overpricing by yurugu's businesses in general (as well as the losses to the mentacidal in exploitative service to yurugu who sell products and provide services to us), entertainment contracts (to include all forms including athletic), car, house, store and credit card interest rates, food, taxation, degrees never intended to be conferred and the relatively lower incomes from those conferred, social security payments for benefits not received (as in most Afrikan male workers who do not live long enough to collect any significant part of what they involuntarily contributed through twenty to thirty years of tax withholdings and sometimes whose families cannot collect in their stead), kwk. Utterly destroyed residences, businesses, business sectors/communities and towns/cities must be added to this list. To this very limited listing, Warriors should feel free to add.

Also in this larger picture, we have to ask how do you make reparations for all of the children who daily die of starvation on the Continent, a direct effect of the war against Afrikan people which began centuries before they were born? How do you correct for the genetic removal of people from the planet as was done in the Islands and the islands comprising Australia? How do you compensate for the unapologetic killing off of entire groups, and the grand genocidal plans to remove them all? How do you make amends for that? It is not through forgiveness and forgetfulness. At least, that would not be yurugu's way. And yurugu can only understand their way.

If one of their ethnicities were utterly destroyed and genocidally removed from existence, they would exact their kind of "justice," quickly and efficiently. But, even if it took them a zillion years, they would exact more than an equal vengeance. They would find a way to convey the message of the value of their people to them through as immoral an overkill as possible.[134] And the historical record will show that they have exercised their murderous intent against others time and time again.[135]

And, in fact, they used this ploy as a means of killing

countless innocent people in order to freely steal their land and resources. This behavior appears in the historical record too many times for a sane person to fathom the inhumanity of it all. The historical pattern is one where (1) they come seeking "friendship" and assistance, (2) both are sympathetically given from the indigenous people which allows them to occupy land and use resources (including people) in others' spaces, (3) the resources are in some purposeful way willfully, arrogantly and callously disrespected by them (as in rape and/or theft), (4) their hosts naturally retaliate for being severely wronged and (5) yurugu uses this as an excuse to go on a killing rampage against them. In the end, this allows them to fulfill their original intent -- to steal everything in the space of the people who had originally compassionately befriended them.

These insatiably covetous, murderous takers just need a self-serving rationalization to assuage their conscienceless schemes. Well, really, not to soothe theirs. Because, in their minds, these self-serving rationalizations serve as justifications to counter the accusations others make about them being inexcusably immoral. They shield them from being revealed for what they truly are, something they are already clearly aware of and have absolutely no problem with being.

This pattern of encountering others, misrepresenting themselves and wanton betrayal of others' trust, followed by "death, destruction and domination," has been repeated with every group they met as they swept across each continent. The only exception to this rule is with some societies in Asia, where they encountered minds similar to theirs who were able to see them coming.

However, this is not a discussion about the murderous rage of europeans in "retaliation" for a just response to an unjust invasion or other violations of others' space, people or way. The details of that would take too many volumes to record. It is enough to say that they are aware of themselves and what they have done. As long as they know, and

Warriors know that they know, it is enough to prepare and not be deluded by any alterations in yurugu's politics designed to change their image into something more human, thereby helping us forget what they owe.

Now that they have finally begun to realize that they are losing their stranglehold over this planet and the minds of those they have done everything in their power to systematically destroy, they are placing a good deal of their energy into making themselves appear human. Defensively putting on an act for the world, they are trying to dissociate themselves from their ancestors (as if the "death, destruction and domination" ended with them) so they can be made to appear innocently fallible and not the inheritors of their ancestors' barbarities. It is an effort to remain in an advantaged position while starting their relationship with humanity on a clean slate so that they will not have to suffer for what they have done.

Warriors know better. We know that we are our Ancestors and we know that they are theirs.

> What about the good white people? Do the sins of the father transfer to the son. **YES!!** The son is the father. The daughter is the mother. The children are the parents, the grandparents, the very progenitors of the racial-phylogenetic-phenotypic-cultural type.[136]

However, like the metaphorical tree that falls in the forest without anyone hearing it, if there's no one to accuse them, then, in their minds, they become innocent. Without anyone to hear the tree, it did not fall. Therefore, in their twisted, self-serving reasoning, without anyone to blame them, they did not commit this worst of all human atrocities.

They believe that through modifying history in this way, that they can erase the ramifications of what they have done. They believe that in convincing everyone else to act as if the chaos they have created is not their fault they will not be seen for what they have done and continue to do. It is their goal to make their destructive way our or everyone's behavior. Or, if that's not possible, they at least would wish to have us believe that what they have done and continue to do is what everyone else would naturally have done or do if they had been afforded the same "intelligence" and opportunity. Once this historical slight of hand is fully accomplished, they will no longer have to stand accused.

If they can make themselves into a people who do not have this type of behavior as a natural part of their character they will be free from the threat of righteous retaliation, not only from others but self-persecution as well. Assuming, as they do, that there is no Creator (or, at least not one who they will not eventually be able to outthink) or Universe to exact judgement, they will be able to get away with what they have done and continue to do. This thinking should not surprise us. It is a logical plan for a god-vying, despiritualized mind.

In the face of the retribution universal order will necessarily reap upon them, an escape route formed through humanity's forgetfulness is their best hope to avoid justice. Obviously, in order for this delusion to become real in its consequences in their minds, they require our complicity.

As a closing thought, Warriors have to ask some very, very serious questions before proceeding with any reparations agenda that will support our movement toward Afrikan sovereignty. Until this offense against the Universe is completely rectified, there can be no peace, at least not for serious Warriors. And until it is corrected in such a way that other people dare not touch us, dare not touch our children, our Way, until we are in a position to ensure that, then no amount of money is going to do us any good in the long run.

As yurugu has repeatedly done in the past, and continues to do today, they can come and take our money, at will. They can come and take our homes by eminent domain or any number of ways. We neither control nor have any real access to their banking industry or any of the financial records kept about us there. Accounts are frozen at their command. We do not operate their information system. It belongs to them. And what this means, in the simplest of terms, is that any one of us can easily be made to disappear on paper (or otherwise) and there is nothing that person, or those who support him or her, will be able to do about it except complain and, that, only in an approved fashion. The same insecurity applies for our cars, our children, our food and anything else we are foolish enough to believe ourselves to "own," including ourselves. yurugu does not need our permission or approval to do what they do against us.

Regardless, Asase Yaa (Mother Earth), the world on which we have been allowed to live in the physical Universe cannot continue as it is. It cannot permanently continue to progressively regress in this direction, damaged and worsening because of the waves of chaos set in motion by arrogant, incomplete, spiricidal[137] beings desperate to turn the All into a mere reflection of their twisted interpretation of reality.

History clearly demonstrates the ineffectiveness of wishful thinking. Prayer for divine saviors to bring universal peace and love, sacrificing our loved ones to the gauntlet of this dehumanizing reality and closing our eyes and ears to the destruction raging all about us have never worked to stop or reverse the ills yurugu has continued to bring into existence since its inception. It is more logical to grasp the timeless truth in the statements "...we are the saviors we've been programmed to wait for and worship"[138], "a thieving spirit cannot be appeased by sacrifice"[139] and "a blind person does not show another the way."[140] A determined, evil energy is real and has no reason to stop of its own accord.

yurugu is yurugu. They will continue in the only way they have ever known. They will, without provocation, and in their characteristically vicious, heartless fashion, do all in their power to dominate, exploit and kill anyone (and anything) who is not them and will stop them from doing so.

Warriors, of course, are our truest Ancestors. And, as such, we have a Creator-given responsibility to correct whatever brings disorder into the human reality. We stand on the frontline as the articulators and "collection agency"[141] of our people. We know how and what to demand, with the backing of mind and power to collect from all, murderers, exploiters and thieves alike, that is due our people.

We remember the human model of civilization we so cherished and earnestly practiced. Therefore, we know that humanity must be returned to its human state in order to truly live.

For this reason, we will continue the righteous work of confronting, by any and every means at our disposal and in our visionary imaginations, anything standing in our nationbuilding Way. We are re-creating an empowered, impenetrable sovereignty for Afrikan people. To this, we give our lives.

ENDNOTES

[1] *The Choice: The Issue of Black Survival in America*, Silver Spring, MD: Cottage Books, 1971.

[2] This Kiswahili term was presented to us by Marimba Ani, one of our most honored Afrikan centered warrior scholars. The Maafa refers to the entirety of the effort european people have put into trying to destroy the Afrikan continent, Afrikan culture and Afrikan people (even though its inception predates the systematic invasion of the Afrikan continent by Europeans by about 840 years when Arabs began their enslavement of Afrikans for themselves and exportation to China and other points in Asia). The european nation is our focus because they expended by far the greatest amount of energy aimed at bringing about our destruction. Ourstorically speaking, the Maafa is a massive, protracted "crime" against *our* humanity. In fact, to even use the word crime as descriptive of it severely minimizes the devastation it brought to Afrikan people. Holocaust is not even sufficient enough of a word. Be that as it may, the Maafa includes the unprovoked wars of invasion to capture and subdue the Afrikan continent, the violent dispersion of Afrikan peoples throughout it, the missionary efforts to remove us from our spirit, the consciously arrogant undermining of Afrikan cultural activities and sensibilities, the brutal and inhumane capture of Afrikans for enslavement and the removal of Afrikans to other lands, the colonization of Afrikan political systems, the balkanization of formerly peaceable ethnic groups and mass theft of Afrikan resources, the confiscation of Afrikan lands and relegation of Afrikans to infertile soil, the global dehumanization of Afrikans, and the brutalization, rape, torture and murder of hundreds of millions of Afrikans and all the descendants those murdered individuals would have produced. *It is important to note that the Maafa is a genocide in progress.* It did not stop with the official end of our enslavement in the western hemisphere (noting that the enslavement of Afrikans on the continent by Arabs continues to date) or the termination of colonization on the continent through revolutionary warfare (noting that an advanced state of neocolonization still plagues virtually every Afrikan state). The continued efforts of white supremacist society

to terrorize Afrikans into nonexistence and the ongoing psychological effects of our past enslavement (referred to by various terms such as psychic trauma, post-traumatic slavery syndrome, cultural misorientation, mentacide, kwk.), as well as the ongoing ruination of the Motherland under a heartless alien and alienating, paternalistic, capitalistic imperialism, are clear indicators that this has been and continues to be one, indivisible "Great Destruction." We must emphatically note, however, that this definition is not to imply that this atrocity is near completion. On the contrary, it is to provide the broadest picture and give a clear understanding of what happened, and is happening, so that conscious Afrikan people will understand the magnitude of what we have committed ourselves to reverse and, in the process, the traditions and sanity to which we fully intend to return.

[3] Mwalimu K. Bomani Baruti, *Centered: Building Afrikan Realities*, Atlanta, GA: Akoben House, 2009.

[4] Sovereignists are those Afrikan individuals and groups who want our people to become completely liberated from any form of domination by others, empowered to this end through our own volition and consciously independent in every spiritual, mental, emotional and physical way. Most importantly, sovereignists are those who are *doing* all in their power to assist us reach this state of existence.

[5] This is taken from the Ganda proverb "The one who is nearest the enemy, in pursuit, is the real leader." And, "in pursuit," as negroes would misconstrue it in an effort to twist our Ancestors words into an endorsement of their subintegrationism, subassimilation and subamalgamation into whiteness, should not be read to mean that the leader is the one who best apes or lives in closest proximity to enemies.

[6] Unlike history, which is the interpretation of past events as if european males were the creators of human society and civilization and, therefore, as if they should be at the center of our discussions about Afrikan people, ourstory is a telling of the past events in the life of Afrikan people – through the eyes of our men, women and children.

[7] Maulana Karenga (ed.), *Selections from The Husia*, Los Angeles, CA: The University of Sankore Press, 1984, p.77.

[8] yurugu, like caucasian or white, is another name for europeans. Marimba Ani brought this name to our attention when she imparted the Dogon myth of yurugu and titled her magnum opus after it. Also known as the pale fox, yurugu is a severed male spirit or principle. He is incomplete. His female half is absent because of a selfish and childish Creator-vying act. Because he was so determined not to wait for the Creator to finish

creating him, he did not receive his female "side" before arrogantly completing himself. Therefore, it was lost forever, and yurugu will remain forever incomplete, destroying all in his path in an effort to find completion in the only way he knows. This myth helps us understand the nature of the european as a function of a spiritual disconnectedness that is uncorrectable by us or them and, therefore, leaves us with a realistic base from which we can reasonably assess options for solving the problem of his blind, unrelenting destruction.

[9] Bobby E. Wright, one of our most insightful ancestors, in *The Psychopathic Racial Personality*, defined "mentacide" as a form of insanity that leaves many of us thinking out of the mind of the european as if it were our own. It is the state of being psychologically brain-dead and having one's thoughts replaced with alien ones, a state akin to being a zombie. "Mentacide" is derived from the root word *menta*, meaning "mental or thinking," and *cide*, meaning "to kill." "Mentacide" means to kill the mental process, to kill one's normal thought processes, essentially, to kill one's own mind. In that there is still a thought process at work, "mentacide" also means that an artificial, alien collection of thoughts and way of thinking have replaced what has been altogether suppressed or removed. (See Olomenji, "Mentacide, Genocide, and National Vision: The Crossroads for the Blacks of America (An Essay of Commentary)," in Daudi Ajani ya Azibo (ed.), *African Psychology in Historical Perspective and Related Commentary*, Trenton, NJ: Africa World Press, 1996, pp.71-82, Kwabena F. Ashanti, *Psychotechnology of Brainwashing*, Durham, NC: Tone Books, 1993 and Mwalimu K. Bomani Baruti, "Mentacide," in Mwalimu K. Bomani Baruti, *Mentacide and other essays*, Atlanta, GA: Akoben House, 2005, pp.5-10.)

[10] negroes, and negroettes, are those persons of Afrikan descent whose loyalty lies with europeans. These individuals do not see themselves as Afrikan to any degree, except as a hyphenated version, which allows them some degree of psychological protection against their destroyers. negroes have intent in that they are consciously anti-Afrikan, doing all in their power to sabotage any self-determined, empowering PanAfrikan or race-based, politicoeconomic initiative, organization or individual effort. They share a deep and committed state of racial confusion and self-hatred, as well as an exceptionally strong and determined denial of their ancestors against whom they take great pride in committing treason. ("negroes" in Mwalimu K. Bomani Baruti, *negroes and other essays*, Atlanta, GA: Akoben House, 2000, Baruti, *Centered: Building Afrikan Realities*, pp.47-52 and *The American Directory of Certified Uncle Toms*, NY: CBIA & DFS Publishing, 2002)

[11] We should be able to appreciate Kwame Ronnie Vanderhorst's phrasing of this distinction between responsibility and accountability for, as he wrote,

> Am I blaming the white man for the problems in the African American communities? It's not about blaming, it's about the truth! There is an enormous difference between responsibility and accountability; that is, the conditions planned for Africans in America, and the solutions of liberation planned by Africans in America. White supremacy global domination is responsible for the inhumane treatment and racist conditions of Africans historically and presently in America and worldwide. Africans in America are accountable for countering "mentacide" and liberating themselves from these conditions placed upon them, externally and psychologically. In short, responsible? No! Accountable? Yes! (*Rearing African Children Under American Occupation*, Washington, DC: Hotep Productions, 1996, pp.13-14)

[12] We do not mean capacity in the scientifically racist, eurocentric notion of innate ability or lack thereof. We are speaking about one's receptivity to revolutionary, Afrikan centered ways of thinking and being based on their ability to overcome their mentacide.

[13] Mwalimu K. Bomani Baruti, *Message to The Warriors*, Atlanta, GA: Akoben House, 2012, pp.162-163.

[14] Mwalimu K. Bomani Baruti, "Irreconcilable Differences," in Mwalimu K. Bomani Baruti, *Eureason*, Atlanta, GA: Akoben House, 2006, pp.201-241.

[15] Tony Martin (ed.), *Message to the People*, Dover, MA: The Majority Press, 1986, p.105.

[16] Afrisms are truths that Afrikans have ourstorically commonly accepted. While there are truisms that can be found to cross cultural boundaries, the body which is unique to Afrikans, and usually in conflict with european truths, can be considered to be the central body of Afrisms, since Afrisms are conceptually used to illustrate fundamental cultural differences in perceptions of truth and untruth between Afrikans and Europeans. However, the entire body of Afrisms includes both those that distinguish Afrikan truth from european truth and those which are generally shared by the indigenous peoples of the world.

[17] At the most, their mistake is definitional because they confuse power with influence. As I stated in a discussion about negroes in the essay "negroes,"

> [negroes] see influence as their most precious and useful tool. But having

influence is very different from possessing power. "Power is the ability to define reality and have other people respond to your definition as if it were their own." (Wade Nobles, *Africanity and the Black Family*, Oakland, CA: Black Family Institute Publications, 1985, p.107) Influence is not power, no matter how much of it you have. It is influence. It advises the powerful. Influence can be ignored at the whim of the powerful. Influence is dependent on the good will of those you try to convince to change their ways. Power is the ability to have your will pursued regardless of what others want. It is self-interested and self-determining. Others comply with your will because they fear your retaliation or honor your wisdom or mutually respect your space. Specifically in the case of oppressors or would be oppressors, the presence of your power would be understood because your threat has been spoken in a language they can clearly understand. And your interpretation of what they are capable of understanding must be grounded in how they exercise power. negroes have no power. (Baruti, *negroes and other essays*, pp.157-158)

[18] And it is irrelevant whether this is due to our subconscious fears or the systematic exclusion of our presence by western media. Our voices are not there.

[19] Most Afrikans in Western society assume that integration is a two-way process of equal give-and-take. After all our lessons, the "melting pot" delusion is still alive and well in our community. Too many of us also assume that so-called integration is a positive and something that we should aspire to. However, integration is not what has happened. What Afrikans and Afrikan ideas and things that Europeans have allowed to be absorbed into their culture have assumed a lesser or subordinate importance and status, or at least have been given the impression of such. Therefore, in using the word integration, we may be using the correct dictionary denotation but it is the incorrect connotation for Afrikans in the Western reality. That being the case, we need a term that more appropriately fits this reality. *Sub*integration will be used herein to include not only the basic ideal definition of integration but to also include the way in which Afrikans (and those ways and things Afrikan) are introduced and incorporated into (and recognized by), Western culture and society. Be mindful that we are not here speaking of those ancient and traditional Afrikan ideas and things that were stolen and distorted into the foundations of European thought and behavior because those Afrikanisms are not accepted or admitted as Afrikan within European culture, thought or society.

[20] Europhiles are Afrikans who are in love with europeans and their ways.

[21] Lost souls are the unconscious, passive equivalent of negroes. They have serious

problems with the Afrikan centered interpretation of reality, but choose to ignore it rather than attack it. Their lot, as far as individual politics goes, is to seek out the safety of the status quo. They remain busy of quietly being as european as possible without drawing too much attention to themselves. And they make no attempt at self-definition beyond that which their appointed leaders sanction. Because of a lack of awareness of their Afrikanity and an uncritical interpretation of european propaganda, but more so because they intensely fear "rocking the boat," most lost souls will follow wherever negroes or white noise leads them. (Baruti, *negroes and other essays*)

[22] It never ceased. When lulls occurred, they were only because some of their barbaric aggression had to be temporarily channeled into violating other places.

[23] Frantz Fanon, *The Wretched of the Earth*, NY: Grove Press, 1963, p.199.

[24] Laini Mataka, "It's All Right To Let Some People Into Yr Vestibule, But Never In Yr Livingroom," in Laini Mataka, *Never As Strangers*, Baltimore, MD: W. M. DuForcelf, 1988, p.14.

[25] Ptahhotep.

[26] Martin, *Message to the People*, p.107.

[27] Mashingaidze Gomo, *A Fine Madness*, England: Ayebia Clarke Publishing Limited, 2010, p.146. Meda ase piii Afia Serwaa Zakyia.

[28] And, as Afrikans, we cannot even begin to think about sovereignty without reflecting on the genius of Marcus Mosiah Garvey. In order for Warriors to fully grasp the magnitude and depth of Nana Garvey's contribution to the conceptualization and creation of Afrikan sovereignty, the following readings are suggested: John Henrik Clarke (ed.), *Marcus Garvey and the Vision of Africa*, NY: Vintage, 1974, Martin, *Message to the People*, Amy Jacques Garvey, *Garvey & Garveyism*, NY: Collier Books, 1963, Robert A. Hill and Barbara Bair (eds.), *Marcus Garvey: Life and Lessons*, Berkeley, CA: University of California Press, 1987, Amy Jacques Garvey (compiled by), *The Philosophy & Opinions of Marcus Garvey*, Dover, MA: The Majority Press, 1986 (first published in 1923), Rupert Lewis and Patrick Bryan, *Garvey: His Work and Impact*, Trenton, NJ: Africa World Press, 1991, Tony Martin (ed.), *African Fundamentalism*, Dover, MA: The Majority Press, 1983, Tony Martin, *Race First*, Dover, MA: The Majority Press, 1976, Amos N. Wilson, *Afrikan-Centered Consciousness Versus The New World Order*, Brooklyn, NY: Afrikan World InfoSystems, 1999 (esp. pp.13-40), Shawna Maglangbayan, *Garvey, Lumumba, Malcolm: Black Nationalist Separatist*, Chicago, IL: Third World Press, 1972 and John Henrik Clarke, *Notes for an African World Revolution: Africans at*

the Crossroads, Trenton, NJ: Africa World Books, 1991, pp.197-244.

[29] Martin, *Message to the People*, p.34.

[30] For a spiritual people, the Creator, divinity and Universe, as one, serve to guide their definition and creation of reality. For a religious, god-vying people, they (and their historically grounded imaginations) serve as their own measurement of what, how and why to craft reality and the means used to control everything in it.

[31] This deep thinking process is critical to any progress we make toward sovereignty.

> Becoming Afrikan centered thinkers requires that we reconceptualize our reality in Afrikan terms and ways of knowing and doing. As a function of correctly defining and acting as Afrikans, our reality naturally changes. Power shifts and balance returns. It is a process of conscious visualization and activation. Because we think so, it becomes so. Reconceptualization is the process of searching out and/or creating more appropriate terms and, especially, meanings to terms that better fit the logically self-interested, nationbuilding politics of our research and agenda. In refusing to accept being bound by others' self-serving, anti-Afrikan interpretation of reality, we are creating, and applying in our daily lives, a "language of resistance."...As with all concepts, our reconceptualizations have full political intent. Our keen awareness of this fact has forced us to explain these terms specifically as they apply to Afrikan centered thinkers and the Afrikan reality we are intent on remaking in the image of our Ancestors. As people guided by a liberating vision, it is imperative that we identify, define and develop those aspects of culture most relevant to our ReAfrikanized nationbuilding. Done together, we reconceptualize our reality into that of powerful, focused warrior scholars. (Baruti, *Centered: Building Afrikan Realities*, pp.21-22)

[32] An Afrikan centered, working definition of civilization must be greater than the sterile one we accepted in our westernized state of mind.

> ...we must employ the knowledge of our children's treatment in our definition of civilization. The state of civilization should not be measured by the amount or level of mechanical technology a society produces or accumulates. It has been said that whether a society is a civilization or not must be judged by the quality of the life of its women. This should be changed to "its children." We say children because they are the most defenseless of all and dependent on adults for their well-being. The quality of their lives speaks to the character of the society developed by their parents. Therefore, using this definition, if significant numbers of a society's children are starving, homeless, mis- and diseducated, sexually

violated, drugged or otherwise intoxicated, obese, suicidal, incarcerated and on death row, then that is not a true civilization. Obviously, people in love with the West who believe it is civilized are using the wrong indicators for measuring civilization. (Mwalimu K. Bomani Baruti, *Nyansasem: A Calendar of Revolutionary Daily Thoughts*, Atlanta, GA: Akoben House, 2008, Ahinime 31 | October 31)

[33] Mwalimu K. Bomani Baruti, "Retardation," in Mwalimu K. Bomani Baruti, *Clarity and Remembrance*, Atlanta, GA: Akoben House, 2015.

[34] *Seeking the Sakhu*, Chicago, IL: Third World Press, 2006, p.289.

[35] As I explained in *Message to The Warriors*,

> So, when we talk about sovereignty, we are not speaking of the popular "sovereignty movement." That fad is about individualism, about feeling free while still under enemy occupation. We are about nationalism, actually being free as a people which would automatically make us into free individuals. We can quickly summarize this point by contrasting the Occupy and Sovereign Citizens Movements with Afrikan Sovereignty. The Occupy Movement is the scheme of disgruntled europeans who are angry with their parents for creating economic problems that are making their lives difficult. This is no different from their parents anger over the Vietnam War and sexual restrictions on open white sex in the 60s and 70s. These spoiled brats have no desire to get rid of the system. They simply want the freedom to live as they choose under the protection of this system. In other words, they want a larger share of the pie. They have no problem having us believe that this is "our" cause because our numbers strengthen their movement's success. But the Occupy Movement has absolutely nothing to do with us. The Sovereign Citizens Movement among whites is designed to force their government to give them more individual and/or group sovereignty. They simply want to legally do whatever they please. For this reason alone, they argue that this government is illegal. And many of them are quite willing to be violent if threatened by its agents. But, in truth, the goal is not to dismantle the capitalist system or make it more equitable, if that were possible and they remain what they are. They only want to change places with the other whites who profit more from it. The Sovereign Citizens Movement among Afrikans is about these individuals learning about the collection of illegal acts of yurugu's government. It, also, is not an effort to change the european's laws. They only want to use their contradictions against them (e.g., to get rid of debt, be exempt from taxation, claim abandoned/unoccupied property, etc.). These "sovereign citizens" want to become immune from legal prosecution. Of course, in itself, the term sovereign citizen is self-contradictory. You cannot be your own government

under someone else's rule. No society has ever allowed that without falling. In our community, this movement is often spread through tricksters who con weak-minded and/or desperate individuals who are willing to pay ridiculous fees for classes. They believe these lessons will teach them how to declare themselves sovereign. It is a form of reactive, "safe sovereignty." These escapists want to pretend that the openly disrespectful behavior Europeans have historically displayed toward others with impunity somehow does not apply to them. They want to believe that somehow, unlike through *all* of their existence, europeans will suddenly change their character and respect anyone's claims to sovereignty within european occupied and influenced space. Whites have never respected the laws and treaties/agreements they have made with others unless those others had the military power to devastatingly retaliate. They have not even done this among their own. So, why would any Afrikan who is aware that europeans see them as their greatest threat, be foolish enough to believe that they would be respected without a means of enforcing their will? (pp.18-20)

[36] Read pages 33-44 in Baruti, *Message to The Warriors*.

[37] For Afrikans, nationbuilding is the process by which our nation is rebuilt. Nationbuilding involves the social and cultural reorganization of Afrikan people globally toward the reconstruction of the spiritual, psychological and physical Afrikan nation. It is the process through which Afrikan people become sovereignly empowered as a politicized, self-defining and self-directing world people who consciously pursue their interests in the face of antagonistic others. The call of nationhood, and the conditions that brought us to this desperate point in the first place, require that we accomplish this phenomenal collective feat with ourstorical remembrance, to the fullest extent of our capabilities as a people wherever we live on this planet without fear, apprehension or regret over the decision to be Afrikan.

[38] And this would include not having to defer to the imperialistic will of the western controlled United Nations.

[39] *Afrikan-Centered Consciousness Versus The New World Order*, p.62.

[40] Mwalimu K. Bomani Baruti, "Self-Serving Spirituality" in Baruti, *Mentacide and other essays*, pp.103-110.

[41] "Healthy Slaves," Baruti, *Clarity and Remembrance*, 2015.

[42] An excellent read to start this journey toward developing an ideal Warrior-workerhood personality is Tika's *Shaasha Barta: The Book of the 41 Virtues*, NY: iUniverse, Inc., 2004.

⁴³ As we iterated much earlier in our discussion of solutions, what we need to study in resolving our problems is what has already occurred, specifically going back to the source of what has already occurred. Few have expressed this simple truth more concisely than Malcolm X.

> When you deal with the past, you're dealing with history, you're dealing actually with the origin of a thing. When you know the origin, you know the cause. If you don't know the origin, you don't know the cause. And if you don't know the cause, you don't know the reason, you're just cut off, you're left standing in mid-air. So the past deals with history or the origin of anything – the origin of a person, the origin of a nation, the origin of an incident. And when you know the origin, then you get a better understanding of the causes that produce whatever originated there and its reason for originating and its reason for being. It's impossible for you and me to have a balanced mind in this society without going into the past, because in this particular society, as we function and fit into it right now, we're such an underdog, we're trampled upon, we're looked upon as almost nothing. Now if we don't go into the past and find out how we got this way, we will think that we were always this way. And if you think that you were always in the condition that you're in right now, it's impossible for you to have too much confidence in yourself, you become worthless, almost nothing. But when you go back into the past and find out where you once were, then you will know that you weren't always at this level, that you once had attained a higher level, had made great achievements, contributions to society, civilization, science and so forth. And you know that if you once did it, you can do it again; you automatically get the incentive, the inspiration and the energy necessary to duplicate what our forefathers formerly did. (*Malcom X on Afro-American History*, NY: Pathfinder, 1967, p.4)

⁴⁴ The asili is a culture's source. It is the underlying principles and fundamental interpretation of reality in the Universe that guide its formation. And it is the original, guiding imperatives that determine its unique characteristic personality of that culture wherever it finds itself. It is the ideal model of thought and behavior that a culture, through its participants, aspires and continually works to become a perfectly balanced representation/reflection of itself. As defined by Marimba Ani, who eloquently articulated this concept, the *asili* is

> ...the germinal principle of the being of a culture, its essence....[It] is like a template that carries within it the pattern or archetypical model for cultural

development; we might say that it is the DNA of culture. At the same time it embodies the "logic" of the culture. The logic is an explanation of how it works, as well as, the principle of its development. Our assumption then is that the *asili* generates systematic development....it is ideological in that it gives direction to development....Cultural *asili*(s) are not made to be changed. (*Yurugu: An African-Centered Critique of European Cultural Thought and Behavior*, Trenton, NJ: Africa World Press, 1994, p.12)

[45] A people's culture is both their creation and explanation. The evidence of it tells us how they see themselves and who they are. Generally speaking, a culture can be defined as everything manmade, material and nonmaterial, passed on from one generation to the next, that is designed to ensure the physical, mental and spiritual survival of that people. It provides the framework, the social mind and personality, by which a population of people who historically see each other as family can interact in mutually beneficial ways, providing for and protecting themselves from antagonistic, external forces. Among a whole host of other things, culture is everything from the rules which govern relationships between individuals and groups within that people to how those people see and interact with those they consider outsiders. It makes them one. And culture, as a social product that takes on a self-sustaining life of its own, is the "invisible hand," the common mind that guides the direction and manner in which mental and material technologies develop that operate to produce, collect, distribute and protect the resources/interests these people consider essential to their well-being. It brings and keeps a people together on a mission of survival and enhancement. All the things which make any people a unique people, even when other people exhibit some similar social characteristics, are qualities of their culture.

[46] "Mentacide: The Ultimate Threat to the Black Race."

[47] Martin, *Message to the People*, p.101.

[48] Depending on the term you prefer, both wholistists and synthesists can be defined as those who look at the Universe and all in it as one. Scientifically, they study the connectedness, not disconnectedness, of all things, including the inseparableness of spirit and matter. They believe in seeking out the forces which operate to functionally interconnect the material and nonmaterial.

[49] There is a clear distinction between educators, teachers and programmers, something of which there is great confusion within the Afrikan community today. *Educators* are those who give knowledge and wisdom knowingly within an Afrikan centered context.

Educators not only teach our children how to think but lead them to understand their power and the responsibility of that power to the Afrikan community. Self-interested, self-defining politics are at the heart of the instruction our educators give our children. *Teachers* are those who simply give information, although this information is inherently, eurocentrically politicized. Such individuals may even present the image of being Afrikan centered, but they are not. Yaa Asantewa Nzingha, one of our proven revolutionary educators, leaves no doubt as to the existence of this confusion in her statement "Reparations + Education = The Pass to Freedom" (in Raymond A. Winbush, *Should America Pay?*, NY: Amistad, 2003, pp.299-314). *Programmers* are the least of what our children need. These instructors do not even understand the vocation of teaching. These nonthinking individuals simply exchange income for spoon feeding us what they have memorized or reviewed overnight without analysis or consideration. They have no knowledge or concern, either way, for the needs of our children or nation.

[50] "Education and Schooling: You Can Have One Without the Other," in Mwalimu J. Shujaa *Too Much Schooling, Too Little Education*, Trenton, NJ: Africa World Press, 1994, pp.9-10.

[51] Ibid, p.15.

[52] *Nyansasem: A Calendar of Revolutionary Daily Thoughts*, Oforisuo 7 | April 7.

[53] And, when we do speak about their formal education or credentials, we have to remain cognizant of who validates them and why. See the "Validation" essay in my *Notes Toward Higher Ideals in Afrikan Intellectual Liberation*, Atlanta, GA: Akoben House, 2006, pp.9-74 and Mwalimu K. Bomani Baruti, "Credentialism," in Baruti, *Clarity & Remembrance*.

[54] Ptahhotep.

[55] Sankofan is derived from the word Sankofa. Sankofa is one of the many Adinkra symbols of the Akan people of West Afrika. It literally means "go back and fetch it." The Sankofa symbol, drawn as a bird with its head turned toward what is behind it, is designed to remind us that we have to investigate and understand our past in order to correctly interpret the present. With this wisdom we can then make determinations as to which direction we should move in the future so that we will be guided toward our traditional ways of thinking and doing.

[56] Mwalimu K. Bomani Baruti, *IWA: A Warrior's Character*, Atlanta, GA: Akoben House, 2010, pp.220-221.

[57] Watoto is the KiSwahili word for children.

[58] In his essay "CIBI's Work," master educator Mzee Sanyika Anwsye draws clear lines of distinction between the politics of those independent educational institutions which rear our children to be Afrikan and those which simply raise them to be american.

> Our children must know, and we must remind ourselves of the difference between African education and that which simply purports to be African education – particularly that offered by charter schools or other such operations funded or conducted, and thereby controlled, by non-African organizations, corporations or governments. Though some brothers and sisters in these programs are well-intentioned, and some of these programs may display African symbolism, use our vocabulary, and justifiably boast of 'academic achievement,' 'character education,' and the like – even 'pride in our heritage' – a fundamental, ncontrovertible difference exists between these sometimes 'African-themed' institutions and 'African [centered]' institutions...That fundamental difference lies in our purpose. As we move forward we must advance that purpose and stop comparing ourselves to other schools. We are not other schools. We are teaching something we have been taught against learning. We are not just teaching our students about Africa – we are teaching them to be African. More specifically, we are preparing workers and warriors to re-establish Righteous Living and full African Sovereignty. We are not teaching our watoto to become patriotic citizens of America or any other non-African, anti-African polity or assemblage. In fact, we are teaching them just the opposite. Charter schools cannot say that, nor can they do that. It is unlikely (read: not possible) that an American government (or its subsidiary state or local governments or corporate affiliates) would fund an operation teaching children to be the opposite of itself. Simply put, if it doesn't meet the strictures of the plantation, the non-African will not fund it. If it does meet the strictures of the plantation, it's not African education anyway.

Along with Mama Makini, his wife of 40 years, Mzee Sanyika Anwisye established the Hofi ni Kwenu Academy/Douglass Institute in St. Louis, Missouri where they have been successfully opening up our children's minds to their Afrikan selves for the last 40 years also.

[59] Pp.101-103.

[60] *Kindezi: The Kôngo Art of Babysitting*, Baltimore, MD: Imprint Editions, 1988.

[61] For a concise explanation of Afrikan complementarity, see Mwalimu K. Bomani Baruti, *Complementarity: Thoughts for Afrikan Warrior Couples*, Atlanta, GA: Akoben House, 2004.

[62] Genocultural is the term used in reference to cultural traits that are genetically

encoded in a people. In terms of those areas where people do have choices, genetics, beyond basic instincts, is culturally bound. It has yet to be accepted by the European scientific community that most thought and action they claim to have a biological origin were molded within a cultural genetic structure. And culture is molded within an asilic (see endnote 44) genetic structure. One could even say that the asili is the mind, and culture is the materialization of that mind. When we use that description and our basic common sense, culture can be recognized as a living entity. So there is no reason to believe that it, any less than any other living thing, does not have a genetic makeup. Beyond the elemental drives of seeking water, food, warmth and shelter, the human genetic structure evolves from a people's adaptation to their social and physical environment. Habitual behavior comes from the refinement of adaptive strategies which, in turn, become biologically locked into the genes. When a people have done something in a particular way for uncounted generations, it becomes natural, it becomes genetic. And, as culture evolves, human biology (genetics) adapts. (See Mwalimu K. Bomani Baruti, *Homosexuality and the Effeminization of Afrikan Males*, Atlanta, GA: Akoben House, 2003, p.125.)

[63] Kofi Asare Opoku, *West Afrikan Traditional Religion*, Accra, Ghana: FEB International Private Limited, 1978.

[64] Tosu Tosasolim, Ason Ajinaku and Marimba Ani, Eighth Annual Abakosem Sunsum program, May 7, 2011, pp.13 and 14.

[65] This concept of "assistance" necessarily requires further elaboration because, in this reality, Afrikans are socialized to await salvation from others and/or elsewhere. In an earlier discussion of Ayi Kwei Armah's book *The Healers*, I talked about a rule which those seeking to be healers must follow which

> ...cautioned against calling on their gods to destroy anyone...[and matches] the 27th Oracle of Ma'at which says *I will not utter curses, except against evil*. To curse someone, or a people, is to call on divinity to bring justice, whatever divinity feels that justice entails. To do so is not wrong if life is at stake and correcting the aggressor is beyond the healer's known ability or power. "Curses are the antidote for curses." Of course, we know the psychological dependency many Afrikans have developed of waiting on divinity to do our work. It is a classic descriptive of how religion is practiced among the truly vanquished. Sadly, many of the initiated and uninitiated in our community have carried this same mentality into their practice of Afrikan spiritual systems. But those of us who recognize that we are at war should know better. Healers are always the first warriors in times of chaos.

> Warriors, themselves, are healers. Therefore, they call on divinity to assist their charge, not fulfill it. Therefore, warrior healers should never call upon their gods to destroy anyone needing punishment that they are capable of correcting themselves. *(IWA: A Warriors Character, pp.141-142)*

[66] Neither the priests nor the Warriors they have been called to guide into their rightful spiritual power should resemble most of those who claim to represent our Ancestors' will today. (Baruti, "Self-Serving Spirituality")

[67] *The Healers*, Popenguine, Senegal: PER ANKH: 2000 (first published in 1978), p.100.

[68] ReAfrikanization is the process by which Afrikan consciousness is deliberately restored by Afrikans. It involves the unrelenting struggle to embrace an uncontaminated Sankofan return to our cultural roots. ReAfrikanization only comes about as the result of a serious, lifelong submersion into the study of our ancestral Way and our evolving, practical, applied rebirth within it.

[69] Certainly, population size dictated that select individuals be appointed and given the authority to represent the interests of their villages, districts, regions or territories and speak on their behalf in larger political decision-making forums. But a deep sense of accountability to their constituency was always embedded in their thinking. This is absolutely not the case for Afrikans under yurugu's domination, whether yurugu is physically present in these spaces or not.

[70] In relation to our ideology and its fundamental need for a sovereignist social theory, I would agree with Bobby E. Wright's statement that

> A social theory determines the destiny of a people by establishing guidelines of life, e.g., it defines their relationships with other living things, it defines values and rituals methods of education, how enemies are to be dealt with, etc. The ultimate achievement of a Black Social Theory would be the recreation of Black culture. ("Mentacide: The Ultimate Threat to the Black Race")

Shawna Maglangbayan's definition of ideology can also assist Warriors in using this concept to frame our sovereign vision.

> The absence of our own revolutionary ideology is the dilemma confronting the Black world. It is not the ingredients for such an ideology which are lacking. Ideologies are not inventions, nor are they the product of "geniuses" or so-called exceptional minds. In essence, an ideology is a set of principles drawn from the

historical experience of a given people, a people submitted to the same general social, economic and cultural realities, in a common historical situation. An ideology can also have revolutionary or reactionary aims; it can be for oppression or for liberation from oppression. If it is revolutionary, the aim of this set of principles is to explain to this given people the causes of their past situation and their present situation, and the ways and means to bring about a future situation consistent with their desire of an independent and free existence. Ideological principles come about through research. Once they have emerged through research and are correctly put together in a coherent whole, they serve for action. Briefly, then, an ideology is a set of principles drawn from the historical experience of a particular people and, as such, it provides the guidelines for action, for change, in the direction desired by that people. (*Garvey, Lumumba and Malcolm: National-Separatists*, pp.109-110)

[71] Erriel D. Roberson (Kofi Addae), *Reality Revolution*, Columbia, MD: Kujichagulia Press, 1996, pp.110 and 111.

[72] Mwalimu K. Bomani Baruti, "Political Paths," Mwalimu K. Bomani Baruti, *Notes Toward Higher Ideals in Afrikan Intellectual Liberation*, pp.76-123.

[73] Mwalimu K. Bomani Baruti, "Black Capital," in Baruti, *negroes and other essays*, pp.99-114.

[74] Hill and Bair, *Marcus Garvey: Life and Lessons*, p.256.

[75] *Iwa: A Warrior's Character*, pp.211-218.

[76] Akoben is the Adinkra symbol which calls people into preparedness for war and to begin hostilities. In *The Adinkra Dictionary* (Washington, DC: The Pyramid Complex, 1998), W. Bruce Willis explains it thusly:

> **Akoben** (the war horn) is a symbol of readiness of war, or a call to action. The war horn was usually an ivory horn with an opening cut at the smaller end. It was side-blown and made a low, loud, earthly sound. In precolonial days, an Akan village and its surroundings might constitute a very large area. Tending crops in the field or in the nearby forest chopping wood, the people might be scattered throughout the village during the course of a day. Because the defense of the town was a collective and voluntary act of the townspeople, the *akoben* alerted the townspeople that an enemy was near or that they should assemble for a task for the common good. Thus, the sound of akoben was a battle cry and a call to arms. In modern times the symbol has been associated with the a state of readiness for a common task, a common endeavor or communal unity for the common good. (p.67)

The recognition that our children and nation are under assault is the reason why our publishing company is named Akoben House and our homeschooling program, adult evening classes, internet classes and educational outreach activities comprise Akoben Institute. We must also note that it is our gradual, progressive mentacidal insensitivity to being destroyed that we, "in modern times," have lost sight of the fact that the enemy has never left the vicinity and the threat remains and, because of this, either are not blowing the Akoben Horn or are blowing it for the wrong reasons.

[77] *When Africa Awakes*, Baltimore, MD: Black Classic Press, 1997 (first published in 1920), p.18.

[78] *Congo My Country*, London, England: Frederick A. Praeger, 1969, p.173.

[79] It is imperative that we define the designed and actual purpose of yurugu's institutions and agencies correctly. Therefore,

> [Warriors] must define "criminal justice system" to fit a conscious, warrior mentality. There is no need to change this term, only its working definition. For us, the western justice system is *criminal*. It is a *criminal* justice system. It is the creation of the white supremacist mind and, therefore, has been molded to fit its anti-Afrikan interests. So, when we use the term "criminal justice system," it is an indictment. The adjective "criminal" is descriptive of the nature of their justice system relative to us. "Criminal" stands alone as the defining adjective, it does not work in concert with "justice" to describe "system." It works alone as an adjective to modify "justice system," explaining its character. (Mwalimu K. Bomani Baruti, "The Hunt Is On," in Baruti, *Mentacide and other essays*, p.18)

[80] Cheikh Anta Diop also provides a comprehensive list in his book *Black Africa: The Economic and Cultural Basis for a Federated State*, Trenton, NJ: Africa World Press, 1987, pp.88-89.

[81] This would be the most difficult for many to comprehend and embrace the possibility of as a sovereignty absolute. However, given the fact that we are being warred against, just in terms of sheer survival, the military option is not optional. And, regardless of odds, Warriors have to think accordingly. Those who say we cannot win because of yurugu's military might do not want to win, at least on sovereign, Afrikan terms. The Ancestors said that, "slaves deserve slaves for children." And those (to include those claiming to have a working knowledge of who we are) whose fear of revolutionary pain is

driven by a historical and ourstorical ignorance of what a dispossessed people (or a determined, organized, skilled, concealed cadre of them) are capable of against seemingly insurmountable odds are no more than vanquished subintegrationists at heart, hoping against hope to turn yurugu into the lovers they cannot possibly be. Certainly, in open warfare, whether spiritual, intellectual or physical, you can expect massive casualties. But casualties are different in meaning and motivational effect when you are fighting a war versus simply being warred upon.

[82] "Kwk" stands for "katha wa katha" and is the Kiswahili term for "etc." ("et cetera") or "and so on." (See the "Abbreviated Glossary" in the front of Kwame Agyei and Akua Nson Akoto, *The Sankofa Movement: ReAfrikanization and the Reality of War*, Washington, DC:)yoko InfoCom Inc., 1999.)

[83] *Notes for an African World Revolution*, pp.7 & 18.

[84] John Henrik Clarke, *Christopher Columbus & the Afrikan Holocaust: Slavery & the Rise of European Capitalism*, Brooklyn, NY: A&B Publishers Group, 1993, p.91.

[85] One of the great myths of the Civil Rights Movement was that we could buy our way out of oppression and into yurugu's heart. However, as Amos N. Wilson pointed out in his discussion of the tenets of Garveyism,

> Ultimate freedom and independence is founded on production, upon the creation of employment, upon the creation of labor and the creation of products for our own consumption. When we look in the world today, we will see that the powerful nations and people are producing people, not consuming people. As I've often said, you cannot consume yourself into equality; you cannot consume yourself into power. Those nations who depend upon consumption will see as they consume the products of others and do not produce themselves, that they will be consumed by others. (*Afrikan-Centered Consciousness Versus The New World Order*, pp.55-56)

[86] Olders are those mentacidal individuals who have done no more than grown old in our neighborhoods. They have consciously worked to subvert the nationalist path either by direct action or an inactive apathy or contempt. Elders have always been there for us. They have lived and will die for us. Nonetheless, even the talents of aging Afrikans who have contributed nothing of worth to the frontline, or have even done all in their power to undermine and dismantle it, should be acquired in this nationbuilding process. It is their skills we need. There is no reason why their politics have to accompany them.

[87] Ma'at is the Kemetic goddess of universal harmony and justice. She also represents the principles of truth, righteousness, reciprocity, balance, order and propriety. As a force in the Universe, Ma'at is the progressive, generative spirit that constantly moves and organizes all life toward equilibrium within itself and in relation to others. (See Jacob H. Carruthers, *Mdw Ntr: Divine Speech*, London: Karnak House, 1995 and Maulana Karenga, *Maat: The Moral Ideal in Ancient Egypt*, NY: Routledge, 2004.)

[88] Listen to Brothas Keepa's libation at https://www.youtube.com/watch?v=RPeJptagfvk. Also see the libation given us by Kobi K.K. Kambon (*The African Personality in America*, Tallahassee, FL: NUBIAN Nation Publications, 1992, pp.189-191 and Mfundishi Jhutyms Ka N Heru Hassan K. Salim, *Spiritual Warriors are Healers*, Brunswick, NJ: Kera Jhuty Heru Neb-Hu Publishing Company, 2003, pp.202-205).

[89] Octavia Butler eloquently captures this truism in saying "The only lasting truth Is Change." (*Parable of The Sower*, NY: Four Walls Eight Windows, 1993, p.3)

[90] Some who understand the asili concept know that this began far before that. Like ours, yurugu's asili has always been with them.

[91] Warriors are healers. This should be understood. The Warrior's role is to do whatever is necessary to bring peace back to his or her people. The Warrior's role is to heal, heal his or her people. However, while some have chosen (in their personal weakness as adult males or females but with a burning desire to still be seen as Warriors) to misconstrue it, when we speak of Warriors as healers, we are not defining Warriors along pacifist, compromised lines. Warriors are not punks, drifting off into some never, never land of embracing all of humanity (including enemies) or self-serving spirituality (which allows them to ignore their primary duty and responsibility to Afrikan people). There is only one way to characterize Warriors as healers in the context of war, and that is of them standing tall at the head of the frontline doing all in their power to stop enemies from harming their people and, therefore, healing them from whatever destruction they have and may experience at alien hands. Healers, like priests, must be reconceptualized in Afrikan Warrior terms.

[92] Geologic time is time considered in enormous chunks. Time, in this way, is measured according to the phases of the geological development of this planet. How much time it took for the continents to separate from one massive land mass as in the continental drift theory is a good example of this type of measurement. While the life of humans is measured in single years and decades and, for some in ancient times, centuries, and that of some insects by hours or days, geologic time is measured in million-year

increments.

[93] Trenton, NJ: Africa World Press, Inc., 1996, pp.428-429.

[94] Another point to note relates to "those particular jobs." There is the mistaken assumption, because it is almost never addressed in the theories or calculations, that these occupations were chosen by our Ancestors. And this is something which wrongly assumes and quietly supports the "happy slave" thesis. There is no consideration in those monetary reparations calculations that there should be reparatory compensation for our enslaved Ancestors' utter absence of occupational choice. In addition, the fact that most of those of us who came were greatly skilled in one area or another is not taken into consideration. There is no differentiation in income taken into account between those who worked the fields, did domestic work in the houses and attended to the handyman tasks in everything from horse/animal husbandry to carpentry to metalwork to other forms of construction.

[95] Quasi-free means to be only partially free.

[96] We use "*en*mate," rather than "*in*mate" because of the distinction we make between our Ancestors who were held captive as laborers by europeans during the Maafa. We do not use the word "slaves" because it carries the meaning of people who accepted their lot as normal and did not constantly rebel against being held in this inhumane, illegal system. We say "enslaved" because that connotes rebellion. It speaks to those Afrikans who might have been physically bound but who never accepted others' definitions of them as inferior and fit to be slaves. It would seem that this same logic should apply to the word "enmate" versus "inmate." Therefore, *en*mate is the term used to distinguish conscious Afrikans locked behind bars by the world's biggest criminals for a crime they may or may not have committed. Naturally, the same logic applies to *en*carcerated and *em*prisoned.

[97] Charshee C.L. McIntyre in *Criminalizing a Race: Free Blacks During Slavery,* NY: Kayode Publications, Ltd., 1984.

[98] Molefi Kete Asante

[99] "Slaver" was a common name for those ships which carried cargos of enslaved Afrikans across the Kemetic Ocean. The Kemetic Ocean is what we now call the Atlantic Ocean. We unapologetically make this declaration using our Afrikan reason. european "old world" maps label the Atlantic Ocean as "Oceanus Aethiopicus" (Ethiopian Ocean). Ethiopian was a Greek label for Kemites (Afrikans) meaning "burnt skin." It is the oldest known Greek word for the Kemites (Afrikans). However, since we are not

these proto-european Greeks or their descendants, we should not use Greek words to characterize and describe the Afrikan reality/worldview. Calling the Kemetic Ocean the Ethiopian Ocean speaks volumes about how the Greeks saw the world. Calling this enormous body of water Afrikan, which means they probably changed it into a Greek name that reflected earlier Afrikans calling it by an Afrikan name, indicates both the respect that Greeks had for the names Afrikans had given to places in the world, as well as the fact that Afrikans had already named this world. Therefore, moving back in time to our original thinking, if anything, we should call the ocean that changed from being the Ethiopian to the Atlantic (also a european(ized) term) nothing other than the Kemetic Ocean. This would be ourstorically consistent.

[100] Dungeons are the names that we give what europeans and misguided Afrikans call the fortresses we were packed into along the coast of Afrika in preparation for transportation to the western hemisphere. The memories from these places are the worst of our "journey" here. More of us died/were murdered in these horrific places than the coffle lines which took us there or the slavers which transported us to the western hemisphere. See Mwalimu K. Bomani Baruti, *Kebuka!: Remembering the Middle Passage through the Eyes of Our Ancestors*, Atlanta, GA: Akoben House, 2005, pp.15-19.

[101] The coffle lines were the collections of Afrikan men, women and children who were held together by ropes and/or chains in groups as we were being marched from our point of capture to the dungeons. See Baruti, *Kebuka!: Remembering the Middle Passage through the Eyes of Our Ancestors*, pp.7-11.

[102] So-called liberal europeans are not exempt from this mentality. Andrew Hacker made this point about even the most liberal of them in relation to education, something most people have already agreed should be made available through tax dollars to all children, especially those who are economically disadvantaged.

> What often distinguishes liberals from others at the same economic level is their greater willingness to pay for programs aimed at resolving social and racial ills. To that extent, then, they seem ready to share some of what they have with others less fortunate than themselves. In this respect, liberals like to feel they are altruistic, and justified in criticizing conservatives for being tightfisted, if not downright selfish. At the same time, the new taxes liberals tend to propose are unlikely to be so severe as to reduce their own living standard in a serious way. (NY: Charles Scribner's Sons, *Two Nations*, 1992, pp.52-53)

[103] And spiritual questions arise when considering the sperm or egg which was previously extracted from those individuals for future procreative purposes, not to mention the need to examine the extreme discrepancies in the racial and socioeconomic status of those who can and cannot afford this procedure and the cost of perpetual storage.

[104] Chukwunyere Kamalu, *Person, Divinity & Nature*, London: Karnak House, 1998, p.33.

[105] This could be referred to as lineacide. Lineacide is distinct from genocide only in magnitude. There are countless occurrences of lineacide (the killing off of sanguine-related family lines) within a genocidal process. Lineacide is the primary attrition process that contributes to a final genocide.

[106] We should remember of all places Haiti where the average life span of an enslaved Afrikan from birth, or moment of arrival on the island, to death was seven years.

[107] We can imagine, though, some negro academician trying to ingratiate himself with yurugu by manufacturing a theory explaining why there should be no reparations using the logic that because there is not enough money or resources available to fully do so that, therefore, the debt must be forgiven.

[108] He points out that

> The mortality rate of this sordid traffic was high....one slave in three was killed in raids or on the trip to the coast, and slave merchants lost one out of three of their human cargo on the voyage across the sea. All told, the slave trade was responsible for the death of about 100,000,000 Africans. (*Introduction to African Civilizations*, Secaucus, NJ: The Citadel Press, 1970, p.306)

Chancellor Williams also speaks to this on pages 255-257 in his *The Destruction of Black Civilization* (Chicago: Third Word Press, 1987) where he quotes an account of our march along one of our trails of tears. In a general statement about how many of us died in the Maafa, he states that "for every two million Blacks enslaved over a million died" (p.255).

[109] P.78.

[110] Reconceptualization, as the process of searching out and/or creating more appropriate terms and, especially, meanings to terms that better fit the logically self-interested, nationbuilding politics of our research and agenda, is very important for those of us standing on the frontline because it frames the definitions of our mission to fit our vision. So, we do not want to say "died," even if at their own hands because, no matter

the actual cause of any of our Ancestors' deaths during our enemies' scramble to capture and enslave Afrikan people, yurugu was the catalyst and who benefitted most from our enslavement. We have no reason to euphemistically play into their hands and every reason not to.

[111] We would be wise to consider this in the context of the fact that,

> Eurocentric theorists and historians list the atrocity stories as though they were merely pathological acts of an otherwise healthy culture. And too often, the fact of European imperialism is presented in the liberal tradition, as a destructive tendency in European culture, that can be effectively counterbalanced by the "humanitarian" aspects of its ideology....[However, it] in not in any way peripheral to the main thrust of the culture; it is not merely an aspect among many, unrelated characteristics. It is, instead, a central theme in European behavior with origins in the core of European ideology. White nationalism and aggression, both cultural and economic, are endemic to European culture: embedded in its ideological matrix. (Ani, *Yurugu: An Afrikan-Centered Critique of European Cultural Thought and Behavior*, p.402)

[112] Baruti, *Message to The Warriors*, p.27.

[113] We must be political in all the concepts we use, knowing that all those given to us serve others' political interests, interests which numb our minds to their intentions and aggressions against us and what we could possibly learn about them and who we are as a people at war with those who design the words we use to describe ourstory.

> Many of us recognize that the term "Middle Passage" is no more than a euphemism softening the horrendous psychological feeling that part of the Maafa spent on the Kemetic Ocean naturally brings. We know that for untrained ears it subconsciously feels more like a mundane leisure cruise than the horrid journey that it was. "Middle" in no way connotes the horror Afrikans experienced. It is a neutral word indicating nothing more than location (middle – between Afrika and this land), while "passage" indicates only a place traveled. "Slave trade" is no different. First and foremost, trade indicates equal and/or fair exchange of goods and services. We weren't traded by any economic measure. We were stolen. Theft is not trade. europeans may, from their vantage point, call it trade. They handled both ends of the "exchange," and both sides benefitted (or, rather, as family, they all benefitted, no matter which side received more). So, they can say that they traded with each other. We, on the other hand, should know that this "trade" in no way benefitted us. We were the merchandise. Along with profit, the

> "slave trade's" prime directive was to destroy us and any connection we had with our motherland so that we would slave for others with blind devotion. If for this reason alone, we would be fools to consciously follow their linguistic lead. (*Kebuka!: Remembering the Middle Passage through the Eyes of Our Ancestors*, p.74)

Of course, we equally have issues with the term "slave" in "slave trade." We make the distinction between slaves and people who are enslaved. Slavery is a mental function where individuals see themselves as property of those who control them. Slaves believe in the correctness of their oppression and exploitation and willingly participate in it. Enslaved individuals understand that they are only physically bound. And they are constantly at war against those who attempt to capture and detain them. Afrikans were not slaves. They were enslaved.

[114] John Henrik Clarke, (ed.), *Critical Lessons In Slavery And The Slave Trade*, Richmond, VA: Native Sun Publishers, 1996, p.14.

[115] Again, we must be political in all the concepts we use, fashioning every word we utter in our own interests.

> The Kemetic Ocean is what we now call the Atlantic Ocean. We unapologetically make this declaration using our Afrikan reason. european "old world" maps label the Atlantic Ocean as "Oceanus Aethiopicus" (Ethiopian Ocean). Ethiopian was a Greek label for Kemites (Afrikans) meaning "burnt skin." It is the oldest known Greek word for the Kemites (Afrikans). However, since we are not these proto-european Greeks or their descendants, we should not use Greek words to characterize and describe the Afrikan reality/worldview. Calling the Kemetic Ocean the Ethiopian Ocean speaks volumes about how the Greeks saw the world. Calling this enormous body of water Afrikan, which means they probably changed it into a Greek name that reflected earlier Afrikans calling it by an Afrikan name, indicates both the respect that Greeks had for the names Afrikans had given to places in the world, as well as the fact that Afrikans had already named this world. Therefore, moving back in time to our original thinking, if anything, we should call the ocean that changed from being the Ethiopian to the Atlantic (also a european(ized) term) nothing other than the Kemetic Ocean. This would be ourstorically consistent. (Baruti, *Kebuka!: Remembering the Middle Passage through the Eyes of Our Ancestors*, endnote 24)

[116] Middle Passage is wholly inadequate as a term to describe the atrocity which brought

us from the Motherland to the americas. Because of its definition, the term Ntoreasee Otuko is much more fitting.

> Many of us recognize that the term "Middle Passage" is no more than a euphemism softening the horrendous psychological feeling that part of the Maafa spent on the Kemetic Ocean naturally brings. We know that for untrained ears it subconsciously feels more like a mundane leisure cruise than the horrid journey that it was. "Middle" in no way connotes the horror Afrikans experienced. It is a neutral word indicating nothing more than location (middle – between Afrika and this land), while "passage" indicates only a place traveled. "Slave trade" is no different. First and foremost, trade indicates equal and/or fair exchange of goods and services. We weren't traded by any economic measure. We were stolen. Theft is not trade. Europeans may, from their vantage point, call it trade. They handled both ends of the "exchange," and both sides benefitted (or, rather, as family, they all benefitted, no matter which side received more). So, they can say that they traded with each other. We, on the other hand, should know that this "trade" in no way benefitted us. We were the merchandise. Along with profit, the "slave trade's" prime directive was to destroy us and any connection we had with our motherland so that we would slave for others with blind devotion. If for this reason alone, we would be fools to consciously follow their linguistic lead. Therefore, to view the "Middle Passage" with an Afrikan mind, we will use the Twi (a dialect of the Akan people of West Afrika) term *Ntoreasee Otuko* (pronounced n-tor-ah-ee-see oh-too-koh) to describe this horrific event in ourstory. Literally, *Ntoreasee Otuko* means a "genocidal forced emigration/exile/captivity." This fits the depiction we are seeking because it speaks to both intent and process. The way in which we were captured and brought here was against every fiber of our will and fully intended to destroy all psychological and genetic memory of ourselves. (Mwalimu K. Bomani Baruti, *Kebuka!: Remembering the Middle Passage through the Eyes of Our Ancestors*, Atlanta, GA: Akoben House, 2005, pp.74-75. We are indebted to Obadele Bakari Kambon's knowledge of Twi for this term.)

[117] However, if just the numbers of Afrikans who were taken to the Islands and South America were added in this total (based on 12.5 million Afrikans having arrived alive in North America), the number of Afrikans murdered during this part of the Maafa would come close to doubling. It is estimated that 11 million (this estimate is noted Leonard E. Barrett, *Soul-Force*, Garden City, NY: Anchor Press, 1974, p.41) Afrikans were stolen and brought to the Islands and South America. And, given that the same percentages

for those murdered on the coffle lines, in the dungeons and on the slavers apply for Afrikans wherever they were taken, then the same reverse calculation would apply for them when calculating the totals murdered.

[118] In a way, we can understand why it was not included. As it is, it would turn many against Wright and scare even more away from considering the appropriateness of the concept of mentacide and reparations as he saw them because he wasn't forgiving and forgetting what had been and continues to be being done to us.

[119] His intrepidity, as well as firm intellectual grasp of the timelessness and universality of the law of reciprocity, allowed Khallid Abdul Muhammad to articulate this sentiment so well for us. He said,

> Yes, we want reparations. You've got to pay us for all those years of free labor; the lynchings; the beatings; the rape of our women; the killing of our babies. Yes, we want the money....buildings....land....We want everything you've got. And then we want your blood! Yes, white men, you have to give up your blood too. What you owe us can't be paid in full until you give up some blood too.

The Gandan proverb "he who makes you shed tears, you make him shed blood" makes the same point.

[120] In my essay, "The Hunt is On," the criminal justice system is defined thusly:

> [We] must define "criminal justice system" to fit a conscious, warrior mentality. There is no need to change this term, only its working definition. For us, the western justice system is *criminal*. It is a *criminal* justice system. It is the creation of the white supremacist mind and, therefore, has been molded to fit its anti-Afrikan interests. So, when we use the term "criminal justice system," it is an indictment. The adjective "criminal" is descriptive of the nature of their justice system relative to us. "Criminal" stands alone as the defining adjective, it does not work in concert with "justice" to describe "system." It works alone as an adjective to modify "justice system," explaining its character. (in Baruti, *Mentacide*, p.18.)

[121] Some would argue that these are competent defense attorneys in that their prime directive is to assist in having us locked up.

[122] "The African American Warrant for Reparations: The Crime of European Enslavement of Africans and Its Consequences." Also see endnote 116.

[123] Many are fooled by the image they portray of themselves through what in western

social sciences is called "impression management." We have to recognize them for the "wholly de-emotionalized beings" they are because it is only when some among them slip, revealing their true selves, that they seek a damage control which requires a conspicuous public display of emotional content. And, that, of course, is only imitative of others who have emotional content and is strictly designed for show only. (Erving Goffman used the term "impression management" to describe how individuals consciously manipulate their environment, others and themselves, as if playing a role on a stage, to convince others that they are something they are not for purposes of control and/or manipulation (*The Presentation of Self in Everyday Life*, Garden City: NY: Anchor Books, 1959). As we understand that individuals mirror their people, this concept does have a larger, macro application at the level of people and their society.)

[124] Rhetorical ethic is a term coined by Marimba Ani which exposes political truth for europeans. This is absolutely attested to by the historical consistency of their shameless, systematic, historical use of lies (false words) against others. These lies are intentionally designed to destroy others (their intent) through using their belief in the humanity of all people to manipulate them into believing that europeans are not trying to destroy them. It is the politics of morality, not universal morality, which rules. And in the Western cultural context, morality is purely political. Extreme individualism removes the possibility of a moral base, especially in Western culture, because anything that produces a profit or physical pleasure becomes morally correct. Regardless of the truth of an individual's statement, convincing others of its truth is what is most important. Skill at manipulating others' minds is the ultimate priority. Truth itself is irrelevant. It is set by the winner. So rules are meant to be broken. And because winning is everything, and deception the easiest and surest way to winning in western society, there can be no moral rules, except those arbitrarily given by the winner. It is the master of the lie who wins. For them, a lie is only a lie when one is caught by those with a greater capacity to punish.

[125] The history of the relationship between Afrikans and europeans should tell us that forgetting and forgiving do not even deserve a momentary reflection. It is a lie that not forgiving guilty people gives them power over you. They will hold power over you until you remove them from being in the position to unobstructively wield their power over you. As long as they remain in that dominant position over you, your forgiveness of them is worthless in preventing them from destroying you and all that you represent. "If a fight is not yet spent, one does not intervene to end it" (Yoruba proverb). In fact,

undeserved forgiveness gives them even more freedom to do against you what they will. If we look at the world through the revolutionary lens our Ancestors have bestowed upon us, we will see that the lie that forgiveness releases us from others' power over us only works for those who could not carry the weight of a warrior scholar's spirit anyway. In any truly egalitarian situation, in order for forgiveness to be sincerely granted, at minimum, these five invariable conditions must be met. The perpetrator(s) must:

(1) with the offended fully cognizant of their historical record of veracity, honestly ask for forgiveness. They must apologize, fully admitting that they are guilty of the specified wrongs. If the act(s) were of a people, this apology must come from them as a people. What difference is the apology of a few when the act was collective? Yes, some of them may realize what they have done from their position of privilege, misguided liberalness and/or neediness, but, how is that impactful to us in the midst of our destruction?;

(2) have completely stopped committing the offensive (physical, mental or otherwise) act;

(3) have stopped trying to draw comparisons between their crimes and those of their victims in an attempt to lessen the impact of what they did (as a schoolyard bully cries that he, too, was hit, as if that hit was not a provoked reaction to unwarranted, repeated aggressions);

(4) fully compensate the offended for the immediate pain and suffering, as well as that which was brought about by the offense(s); and

(5) have had their "blood debt" collected by those whose blood they needlessly wasted.

None of these apply to europeans with respect to Afrikans. True repentants apologize for they truly feel remorse for and actively seek to make amends for, give restitution to, and repair the damage done. They do not just pretend that what they did has no meaning, or has produced an uncorrectable effect and, therefore, they cannot and are under no obligation to do anything about it. They *know* they are wrong and act accordingly. Forgetting, of course, is even more nonsensical because forgetting leaves one open for repeated assaults, by the same people, in the same way. Even worse, if you forget your way home, if you forget the destruction which brought you to where you are now, you will not be able to retrace your steps and reverse the process. You will not be able to find your way home. So, even if we rediscover our roots but do not understand what tore us from them, we can easily be ripped from them again and again and again, each time becoming more distant from the possibility of a full and final return. Forgetfulness can be even worse than forgiveness. Sadly, some of us see erasing any non-european sanctioned ourstorical truths and any ongoing atrocities against Afrikan people as critical to sustaining a mentacide we have accepted as our natural state of being. Those Afrikans openly advance an unqualified forgiveness and forgetfulness for the demonic attacks of europeans against us. In fact, blended with a "we're all human" argument, they proclaim that yurugu's penchant for creating havoc and pain must be euroversalized so that their peculiarly aggressive way will not arm those of us with the potential for consciousness with one of the critical tools we need to rightly set europeans apart from others so we can see them for what they are – curstorical knowing and remembrance. This is why these misguided individuals are so accepting of european liberal humanitarians who indicate that they are willing to apologize, forget the past and move on as one. They have found their ideal political mates – an apparently repentant enemy who wants nothing more than their attention, love and appreciation and, in turn, is willing to give them what they so desperately desire, their validation and defense against those of their own who would hold them accountable for their willful treason. To the mentacidal Afrikan made into the stunted shadow of a european liberal humanitarian, this is the ultimate victory.

[126] A very telling example of this is the unbelievably low level of support that we now give to our own businesses. Out of the over one trillion dollars in spending power Afrikans have in this country only 4-6 percent is used in Black businesses. There is no reason to believe that this behavior, and the self-defeating thinking behind it, would change without an extensive re-education of the masses of Afrikan people.

[127] Although only one in a long line of warrior scholars who has identified our insanity as a function of our adjusting to, internalizing and embracing an alien and anti-Afrikan culture as normal, Kobi K.K. Kambon has consistently defined and explained this phenomenon well (*The African Personality in America: An African-Centered Framework*, and *African/Black Psychology in the American Context: An African-Centered Approach*, Tallahassee, FL: Nubian Nation Publications, 1998). As taken from the introduction of his latest effort, *Cultural Misorientation*,

> The European American community's drive to disguise and conceal their culpability and guilt in the destruction and oppression of Africans through their collective-societal institutional arms requires American society (both Whites and

it's Black victims as well) to operate in a kind of "collective psychosis." Everyone appears to operate in a blatant denial of the true history of Africans in America and the continuing contemporary legacy of that history, which allows Whites to feel secure and positive about themselves, and to project themselves to the world as the apex/standard of civility and high culture (with the implied beneficial psychological, economic, political, spiritual, etc., outcomes for everyone). Thus, maintenance of the psychological comfort level of European supremacy in American society requires (or demands, in fact) this kind of collective denial or "psychotic" behavior and functioning among Africans in virtually every aspect of American life. Consequently, the Black race in America is literally forced to, and is reinforced (rewarded/applauded, etc.) for functioning in a state of collective/mass psychosis. Within this context, Africans in America re reinforced for suppressing and/or denying their true racial-cultural identity and history (i.e., their integrity as human beings), for remaining ignorant of their true history and culture in the world, and for internalizing as much as possible of a Eurocentric consciousness. This is, in my view, the ultimate statement of psychological-cultural oppression which is illustrated by the African psychological predicament in America and throughout the world. (Tallahassee, FL: Nubian Nation Publications, 2003, p.1).

Amos N. Wilson has done the same for the concept "other-directedness" in his *Blueprint for Black Power*, NY: Afrikan World InfoSystems, 1998, p.123 and 135. And Kwabena F. Ashanti, has done justice to our insanities in his description of being a "zombie." (*Psychotechnology of Brainwashing*, Durham, NC: Tone Books, 1993, pp.95-96).

[128] Detractors abound. Most would argue that I am going on and on about the atrocities to which yurugu must repay while these Afrikans' deepest sympathies go toward seeking justice for the litany of destructive acts europeans admit to committing against themselves as well as the endless propaganda that terrorist threats from everywhere are waiting in the wings to ruin yurugu's "democracies."

[129] And this naturally brings up the need to calculate for the magnitude of our miseducation and, now, diseducation.

[130] It is understood that, subconsciously, they know better to vent against the source, europeans. Somewhere in their mentacidal haze, they *know* that yurugu will kill for nothing and, especially, if they perceive that "nothing," even remotely, as a threat. negroes and lost souls fear of us is based on seeing us as instigating yurugu's rage against Afrikan people and/or being in our presence during it. In the case of lost souls, though, their fear is for us. They believe we need to be protected from ourselves because we "know not what we do."

[131] Warriors have the option of being officially or unofficially Afrikan by name in western society. Many have chosen to not pay yurugu to have returned to them what was illegally taken using the proverbial Afrikan logic that "it is the fool whose own tomatoes are sold to him."

[132] Ngugi wa Thiong'o, *Matigari*, Trenton, NJ: Africa World Press, 1998, p.95.

[133] Meda ase Marimba Ani for speaking this term into reconceptualized existence.

[134] Among countless others, a well-performed example of this is found in the movie "The Usual Suspects" where the character Keyser Soze, a gangster in old europe, comes home to find his family under siege by three other gangsters. His wife has already been raped, one of his son's throat is cut in his presence and his daughter is being held at gunpoint. To prove his "will" to the three men, he shoots two of them and then proceeds to shoot one of his remaining children, his wife and, then, his other child, the daughter held at gunpoint. He lets the other thoroughly unnerved gangster go as if to warn the other members of the mob what's coming. Then, for those involved in the home's siege, he "kills their kids. He kills their wives. He kills their parents and their parents' friends. He burns down the houses they live in and the stores that they work in. He kills people that owe them money."

[135] This must be contrasted with our mindset through the example of those of us who have falsely spent years in prison and, upon exoneration and a smidgen of financial compensation, if that, do not call for justice (given that those who falsely accused us do not spend a moment behind bars or lose a penny of their income or wealth and, if they did, it would not be commensurate with what they took away from us) but loudly proclaim throughout the media their forgiveness for those who destroyed them. A *criminal* justice system does this to us and we still praise its idea of blind justice. People do this to us and we pray to have their sins forgiven.

[136] Akoto and Akoto, *The Sankofa Movement: ReAfrikanization and the Reality of War*, p.46. And our Yoruba Ancestors tell us that "those who sow the seeds of wickedness, do so upon the heads of their children." The following two quotes also do justice to this point.

> You owe us some bank
> And we ain't talking millions,
> We ain't even talking billions
> We talking trillions
> White folks say why should they have to pay

> For something that was done way back in the day
> What if I came through and I shook your hand
> Raped your women and I took your land
> Put you in chains and made you work for free
> How would you feel, what would you see?
> You inherited the wealth from slavery
> We inherited the poverty.
>
> Stic Man
> "Reparations"

> "If you are the son of a man who had a wealthy estate and you inherit your father's estate, you have to pay off the debts that your father incurred before he died. The only reason that the present generation of white Americans are in a position of economic strength is because their fathers worked our fathers for over 400 years with no pay. We were sold from plantation to plantation like you sell a horse, or a cow, or a chicken, or a bushel of wheat. All that money is what gives the present generation of American whites the ability to walk around the earth with their chest out like they have some kind of economic ingenuity. Your father isn't here to pay. My father isn't here to collect. But I'm here to collect and you're here to pay."
>
> Omowale Malcolm X

The reader is also directed toward Amos N. Wilson's statement on this in his *Afrikan-Centred Consciousness Versus the New World Order* (pp.94-95). We have to remember that the *entire* european nation rose as a result of our enslavement. See Eric Williams, *Capitalism & Slavery*, Chapel Hill, NC: 1994 (first printed in 1944). And, as taken from *Message to The Warriors*:

> ...all europeans, from the materially wealthiest to the poorest, from the newest to the latest arrivals to these shores, reap the benefits of stolen property. The very spaces they occupy and claim as their countries, the places which feed and house them and which they so patriotically protect, were stolen from others. The condition they live in on this stolen property is irrelevant. And, unlike what the media would lead us to believe, the majority do not live in deprived situations, especially in comparison to us or the other people their ancestors murdered in order to steal it. Even their hungry and abused benefit from having pale skin, if not materially then psychologically. Those who receive stolen property, *according*

> *to their very own laws*, are as guilty as those who stole it. There has been an incredible transference of property through their generations. And the value of what was originally stolen has grown beyond calculation. We must also remember that the genocidal method by which it was stolen is also inherited by those who continue to benefit from this murderous theft. The sins of the fathers and mothers are passed down to the sons and daughters. This is universal law. Lineage, the bloodline, is the most important factor tying benefit and blame to the whites we see today. If we understand how lineage works, we know that *they are their ancestors*, just as we are ours. (Baruti, pp.40-41)

[137] Spiricide is the killing or continuous suppression of the existence, connection and/expression of Spirit in human consciousness.

[138] Sadiki Bakari, *Liberation Song: The Book of Resurrection*, 2009.

[139] Ngugi wa Thiong'o, *Matigari*, Trenton, NJ: Africa World Press, 1998, p.102. He adds on page 76, "Give a little sacrifice to appease a thieving spirit, and this will only whet its appetite and greed for more…"

[140] Kikuyu proverb.

[141] Meda ase for the thought Mimi Gal.

Akoben House Order Form

Please send

__ copies of *Sovereignty* ($19.95 each) $_____

__ copies of *Clarity* ($21.95 each) $_____

__ copies of *A Warrior's Love* ($16.95 each) $_____

__ copies of *Message to The Warriors* ($19.95 each) $_____

__ copies of *IWA: A Warrior's Character* ($24.95 each) $_____

__ copies of *Centered* ($16.95 each) $_____

__ copies of *Yurugu's Eunuchs* ($18.95 each) $_____

__ copies of *Nyansasem: Revolutionary Daily Thoughts* ($19.95 each) $_____

__ copies of *Sesh* ($16.95 each) $_____

__ copies of *Eureason* ($19.95 each) $_____

__ copies of *Notes Toward Higher Ideals* ($16.95 each) $_____

__ copies of *Battle Plan* ($14.95 each) $_____

__ copies of *Kebuka!* ($18.95 each) $_____

__ copies of *Mentacide and other essays* ($16.95 each) $_____

__ copies of *Asafo* ($19.95 each) $_____

__ copies of *Complementarity* ($18.95 each) $_____

__ copies of *Homosexuality and the Effeminization of Afrikan Males* ($29.95 each) $_____

__ copies of *The Sex Imperative* ($19.00 each) $_____

__ copies of *Excuses, Excuses* ($17.00 each) $_____

__ copies of *negroes and other essays* ($17.00 each) $_____

__ copies of *Chess Primer* ($12.95 each) $_____

Shipping & Handling: $_____

($6 for 1 book and $4 for each additional book.)

TOTAL ENCLOSED: $_____

NAME: _____

ADDRESS: _____

_____

Send this order form, along with your check or money order (made payable to Akoben Village), to:

Akoben House, P.O. Box 10786, Atlanta, GA 30310

OR order by credit card at **www.AkobenHouse.com**

Made in the USA
Coppell, TX
05 January 2022